In and out of Africa

...in search of Gérard Depardieu

In and out of Africa
...in search of Gérard Depardieu

FRANCIS GIMBLETT

THE WINE ADVENTURER PRESS

In and Out of Africa … in search of Gérard Depardieu

Originally published in Great Britain by
The Wine Adventurer Press

1st Edition published 2009

The Wine Adventurer Press
Jeroboam House, Grayswood,
Haslemere, Surrey, GU27 2DG

Printed and bound by The Choir Press Ltd

ISBN 978-0-9561821-0-4

FOR JOE

Who with each comma, semi-colon
and full stop I write, will ever be my editor.

AUTHOR'S NOTE

Everything within these pages happened, the characters depicted are real, no names have been changed and nothing is fictitious. I hope that I have done enough justice to those about whom I have written for them not to mind any candour. I would like to express my heartfelt thanks to all those Philip and I met on our journey. I also would like to thank Philip himself, without whom the adventure would have been significantly diminished - and deprived of Barry White, which, of course, no adventure should be without.

For the sake of brevity and pace, the story itself touches on the highlights of the wine visits. A fact file appendix has been added for those wishing to know more. This lists all of the visits in order and, in turn, catalogues all of the best wines of North Africa. I hope that this may provide enough to quench the information thirsty.

Out of Africa – England

'Le Faux Pas'

Wine: the liquid picture book that tells its story with every sip; taking you to places unimagined and to times long past, it offers a glimpse of the wondrous worlds of those who toiled to bring it to you. But, as Homer observed when he wrote: 'The wine urges me on, the bewitching wine, which brings forth words which were better unspoken,' it can also get you into trouble …

Had I not been conversing by video link, and instead been in the television studio with Gérard Depardieu in person, I might not have said that nose size was unimportant in relation to wine tasting ability. However, emboldened by separation, I went for the cheap laugh; something I was later to regret. He graciously acted as if he found it very humorous and continued to chuckle as the show's compère, Graham Norton, expanded upon the theme, suggesting that the size of one's nose often correlated with the dimensions of another attribute. I suppose, however, that there's a difference between implying that your large hooter doesn't necessarily make you a good wine taster, and that you might be particularly well endowed. It was only a few moments later that I realised it might have been better to keep the fiery actor-turned-winemaker on side.

1

Having been asked to host a tasting of his new Moroccan wine on the show, I had worried about what I was going to say. This was less because I was going to meet one of my film idols, but rather more because I believed that, coming from Morocco, his wine would leave me straining to describe positively something with the sensory impact of gargling with paraffin ... with a man who knew how to use a box of matches. The few Moroccan wines I had ever drunk had left me in no doubt as to why fuel is cheaper in North Africa.

The moment had come. The studio audience, each equipped with a generous measure, waited expectantly. Gérard put his nose into the glass, breathed deeply and expelled a gentle moan of appreciation; something some winemakers do when trying to influence your opinion. Be nice about the wine, I thought to myself, you're not here as a critic. I tried to think of something positive as I swirled my glass and prepared for the nasal assault. The liquid's cherry colour, turning tawny at the edges, at least looked promising. There's a start, I considered, I'll focus on that. There was no need. As I closed in on the glass I felt my nose enter a sensory vortex, and a myriad of aromas triggered that rare involuntary response when at a wine tasting: a broad smile. (If it occurs at a Masters of Wine tasting, one is in fear of being ejected for being either drunk, or enjoying oneself: the former frowned upon, the latter prohibited!)

I then took a sip. The wine was like reflexology for the mouth, albeit, due to the wine's power, performed by an Amazon. And although it had enough alcohol to put you in fear of a naked flame, if someone had lit a blowtorch under my nose I wouldn't have noticed. The wine was a joy to describe.

Allow me to digress ... Most everyday wines should be

2

described in general terms, such as fruity or floral, etc, because they don't have high concentrations of any particular aromatic. This leads to the disbelief felt by many when watching television pundits describing a simple wine verbosely (in short, yes, they are often talking rubbish). But when a wine has high concentrations of aromatic compounds you can detect individual, and often very pronounced, characters. Sadly these wines cannot be mass-produced, so are harder to find, but not always more expensive.

As I began to elaborate on the wine I expected a lambasting from the forthright host, but even Norton nodded as I mentioned prunes, dried cherry and raisins, likening it to the first bite of a mature Christmas pudding. Gérard added 'sous bois', which I explained was a term used to describe the smell of a forest floor. Norton feigned disgust, but I think Gérard was thinking of herbs in Provence rather than a wet morning in Epping.

The interview was short, and once the wine had been plugged there was no time to ask him how he had coaxed such a good wine from a land with such a poor reputation. I wanted to know more but the show was over before I could arrange an opportunity to talk again. I decided somehow to contact him.

Finding a phone number for his vineyard was more difficult than a search for a Majestic in Mecca, and, once I had, the silence that greeted my messages suggested that maybe I hadn't entirely endeared myself from the outset.

There was nothing else for it, I would have to pack the Land Rover and drive there! Well, there were a few other ways, but I didn't think of them until the times came when I wished I had.

* * *

Whilst my thinking may seem drastic to those who are sound of mind, early in my wine career I had developed a passion for wine travel and discovery bordering on the unhealthy, and, having thought I had explored every corner of the globe that produced the good stuff, this was an opportunity just too tempting to miss.

I suspected however that travelling uninvited to another continent in search of Gérard Depardieu would place me firmly under the category 'stalker' in the eyes of the law, so I decided to broaden the quest. Were there others making such wines? I looked to the internet for winery websites, though there were none to be found. I thought the wine trade directory might provide me with names and numbers, as it had for previous trips, but I could find only two Moroccan wines being imported into the UK: those being the ones on which I had founded my original negative opinion. A glance told me that there was nothing listed for Tunisia or Algeria either, the other two North African wine-producing nations.

My French grandfather had served in Algeria during the war and wine featured in one of his stories, though it concerned the debilitating effect it had on the knees of a tea-drinking platoon of British troops, rather than providing any description of the wine. Under the circumstances, this is an oversight he might be forgiven for. In fact, had he shouted: 'Boys, you must taste this! I'm getting guava, mango, quince ...' I suspect he would have come under friendly fire.

I then dug out my wine books but, other than a few entries explaining in schoolmasterly tones that the three countries 'have potential, but are under-achieving', I found little to assist my search for other good wines. There didn't seem to be much new to the writing though, giving me hope that there might be more recent developments to unveil. What I read of the natural conditions, however, was revealing. Unlike other North African countries not accomplishing much in wine terms, these three have altitude – an important asset for making good wine in hot countries, as it gives rise to cooler regions. They also have other factors that could help them improve, including great soils and old vines. History had once seen these countries as major players too. At one stage, under French control, the three were responsible for over two-thirds of internationally traded wine (albeit mostly destined for the mother country). Their wine was also widely used to improve French wines. A lot of Burgundy tasted differently in the first half of the twentieth century to the second half, after North African Independence. This is something, however, that is best left unsaid in the cellars of Burgundy – it may result in reduced tasting measures.

I could now confidently report that these countries 'had potential but were under-achieving'! Investigative journalism at its finest.

With one arm now firmly thrust into the sleeve of my wine anorak, and intent on driving through all three countries, I wondered how best to go about finding the wineries. It was clear that, whilst permitting wine production to an extent, the respective Muslim governments were not keen to see it advertised, so getting appointments wouldn't be easy. Simply turning up and driving around a bit occurred to me, but I considered this might not be the most clinically efficient way of going about it. The consulates for the three countries would surely have a list of wine producers, I thought.

'We are a Muslim country and do not promote such things,' was the curt reply from a junior within the Tunisian consulate. In fairness, he may have just been frank, though after enduring twenty minutes of computer-generated lute music on hold, any negative response sounds curt.

A very nice lady at the Moroccan consulate eventually found a mobile number for the owner of a winery, which, after having spoken to seven people, began to leave me with a small sense of achievement. But it was a delightful man at the Algerian consulate who began to give me a real feeling of progress. He explained that I would need only one telephone number to see all of the best vineyards in Algeria, as they were all state owned, and he explained how I should go about obtaining a visa. With hindsight, he did seem a little surprised that I wished to drive across the country, though enthusiastically started suggesting a route. I began phonetically jotting down Arabic names that I hoped would later correspond to a map, but when he mentioned taking a ferry to Alicante I questioned his navigational skills. I said surely Alicante was in Spain? He complimented me on my knowledge of geography.

'Why can't I drive to Morocco from Algeria?' I asked. Drawing a breath heavy with wonder at my ignorance, he gathered himself and explained that the border had been closed for ten years. Now wishing that I'd boned up on local politics, I again asked why? He hesitated, no doubt thinking how best to explain this to someone of clearly limited intelligence, before saying, 'It's because we don't get on.' Afterwards something about the conversation made me suspect that I should get a second opinion on my travel plans. Call it intuition.

'I have three words for you,' said an official at the British Embassy in Algiers: 'Don't do it.' Prior to my call I had searched the internet for 'Algerian politics' and what I had read made me suspect that the British government's attitude to a road trip through Algeria would be somewhat less enthusiastic than the Algerian one. By way of explanation the official said that they were having a 'spot of bother with terrorists'. He then said he 'must dash', as he was expected somewhere. As I put the phone down I imagined him leaping onto his charger to round the blighters up.

Disheartened, I contemplated a trip to an Algerian theme night at Center Parcs instead. The thought alone was enough to have me again deciding to take a British-registered Land Rover through a country recently out of civil war, and where the government's opposition had aligned themselves to Al-Qaeda and vowed to attack foreign targets. Surely, our government was being over-protective? Cynical thoughts of the nanny state began to embolden my views when a link entitled 'Insurgency in Algeria' caught my eye on screen. It was a list of recent militant activities that made the prospect of couscous in Nottingham very attractive. The list came capped with advice from the Foreign Office advising not to travel to Algeria unless the journey was essential, and warned of 'small-scale attacks, including bombings, illegal roadblocks, kidnapping and murder in many rural parts of the country.'

In the light of my findings, I felt a compromise might be prudent. I would drive down to Tunisia, then go around Algeria to Morocco and later return to Algeria by plane. (The Algerian leg remaining 'essential' in my estimation.) I considered the options on getting from Tunisia to Morocco. The first route involved a three-week trans-Saharan drive around Algeria, through Libya, Niger, Mali and Mauritania (via Timbuktu!), before crossing into Morocco. The other, a two-day trip back through France and Spain. It was a close run thing, but the European option won.

In the following days I began to have some luck with contacts. A call to the number I'd obtained in Morocco gave me others to follow up, and from there I worked the phone and developed a list of the best producers. When, one morning some days later, I gained my first appointment, I put down the phone and pulled out a bottle to celebrate. The following day I felt that subsequent successes should be accorded less revelry, lest the trip, and I, not make it past the meeting preparation stages.

I began to consider the cost of the quest. A call to my business consultant told me that I'd lose focus on my company and that it would be expensive. I retorted, 'I'll pay for it by writing a bestseller!' His initial response is unprintable, and he continued to explain that agents receive a thousand manuscripts a week but take on only a handful of new writers a year. The earthy language returned as I suggested getting a production company to film it for television. Apparently I'd probably have to pay them, unless I had a track record. My consultant once said the only reason I call is to have someone to ignore. Again he must have wondered why I'd rung, as I thanked him, saying I'd write a book anyway and film the trip myself. I would have to do it on the cheap though, and this led me to thinking of tents and, in turn, bugs, snakes, sweat-lined sleeping bags, matted hair, strip washing and farts. My opinion of them (tents, not farts) was founded largely on my last, not entirely successful, outing. The compromise was to buy a tent that I could fix on the roof of the car, which would at least take care of the bugs and snakes. There'd still be a generous amount of the rest no doubt, though those I could keep to myself – or so I thought.

I started to ponder how I might single-handedly conduct the winery visits, write a book, film a documentary, and drive nine thousand miles in thirty days, when a good friend offered to join me. This, it should be said, came at the end of an evening that involved pulling the corks on a best-forgotten number of bottles. The morning and sobriety brought to light a number of obstacles to his coming (a job, a pre-booked holiday, and his wife giving birth among them), but I decided the idea was a good one and called another friend who had found himself at a loose end after selling a business.

Philip was born on the other side of the world thirty-four hours before me. If I were to have asked a computer to come up with the attributes necessary for an ideal wing-man for the trip, it would probably have said I needed an ebullient, physically fit, optimistic, intelligent, resourceful, gastronomically adept and slightly balding South African who was in need of a new challenge. In Philip I would be short of only one: he had lost a little more hair than that.

* * *

Two months later. It was the day before our departure and we now had appointments with all of the very best producers in each country. All, that is, except one! I still hadn't spoken to Gérard despite tracking down his agent, his winery's representative in England and a florist in Paris who thought she might have a mobile number for him. I was convinced now that Interpol would have a fairly detailed description of me and be monitoring my whereabouts. At one point I had spotted his wine on a merchant's list, though apparently this had been printed before shipment, and the wine had failed to arrive. Maybe it was somewhere with the man himself – had he been seen recently? I suppressed my concerns and returned to packing.

Philip was now on board and had arrived. As he is a meticulously well-organised man, I was pleased that he generally approved of my preparations. He was a little surprised by the level of security I had introduced to the car however, asking whether, in addition to the reinforced storage boxes, pedal locks, immobilisers, extra padlocks and neighbourhood watch sticker, I had made the glass bullet proof.

Having done military service in his homeland, he recognised the rooftop storage boxes I'd bought as South African army ammunition cases – not something mentioned by the seller on e-bay. 'Might they attract the wrong sort of attention?' I said that Africa was a big continent and they would likely use something different in the north. We'd also got hold of some fairly serious camera equipment loaned by a friend in the television business. A day's film training a few days earlier had left us looking almost professional – something we would later spend time convincing men with guns we weren't.

The anticipation of the trip had put the prospect of leaving our families for nearly a month to the back of our minds. The realisation that we now were about to do just that, coupled with the 3am start, gave a subdued air to our departure. As I turned the key in the ignition it struck me that I'd not spent more than four days apart from my wife, Pamela, in fifteen years. Philip must have been in a similar mood as we bowled along an empty M25. The first track he chose from his CD collection, 'Nothing Compares To You', nearly brought a tear to my eye. The next three, by Simply Red, Phil Collins and Barry White, gave me real cause to cry. This was a grave oversight on my part. I had rashly agreed to him preparing the music for the trip. A quick look at the collection didn't settle my nerves. Philip must have detected a critical note in my voice when I asked if his wife had made the compilation, leading him to suggest that anything played through the Land Rover's speakers sounded appalling anyway. He had a point. I was used to my music sounding as if it were relayed via a hosepipe, though I explained that the car was built as a workhorse rather than to pander to those needing a high level of gadgetry, referring to the vast flight-console in his car. It being a hybrid Toyota led to the inevitable discussion about fuel efficiency and environmental impact, to which my parry was that he would put five cars into landfill in the time that mine was on the road. I knew that this was an argument that would only be supported by people with large beards in off-road magazines, so changed the subject. I pointed out a new vineyard adjacent to the motorway, saying that these Kentish vines were about as far north on the globe as grapes for wine can successfully be grown; and we would be travelling to the furthest point south, nearly fifteen hundred miles away. He muttered something about not doing 65 miles to the gallon.

These vines are a part of England's fledgling revolution in winemaking. Planted on chalk, in fact the same layer that Champagne sits on, their grapes are destined for sparkling wine production, which, in my opinion, most winemakers in England would be best doing. I am aware that this will incite derision from most producers of English still wine (though not from as many drinkers), but the climate is best suited to producing thin, acidic wine, which forms a great base for sparkling. They generally don't bother making the non-sparkling stuff in Champagne because it's too cold, so why should we think we could do better even further north? One producer cited global warming as a reason for beginning to make red wine in England; though on tasting his Pinot Noir – the experience not unlike crashing face-first from a bicycle into a patch of nettles ('rather herbaceous', I think he put it) – I decided that the ice caps would have long melted, and his vineyard flooded, before the wine would be drinkable.

This was the nature of our conversation as we handed our passports to customs and queued for the tunnel. We bought a coffee and discussed how to film our lunchtime stopover in

11

Champagne. The talk of wine had us anticipating our first sip amongst the vines, but it soon proved such a simple objective would be well beyond our capabilities.

Out of Africa – France

'I get no kicks …'

I banged on the window. 'Je voudrais du champagne!'

The girl wondered whether she should open the shop door to a long-haired Englishman, who, now a little red in the face, seemed less sanguine than the normal champagne buyer. I dropped my shoulders, took a deep breath and smiled. As she had only just closed for the afternoon she generously unlocked the door.

The shop was little more than a corridor, the walls of which could not be seen from ceiling to floor for packets of dry goods. Wafts of synthetic Nordic forest from a stack of washing powder mingled with the smell of musty cardboard. The girl quietly stood by the door, still unsure as to my motives for demanding alcohol in such an insistent fashion. I strode towards a far shelf. There sat a familiar bottle shape, only one, but by now I wasn't interested in choice.

On drawing up our route south to Marseilles and the weekly ferry to Tunisia, the pen didn't have to wander too far to take in three of France's greatest wine regions: Champagne, Burgundy and the Rhône. Whilst the Champagne region would bear little resemblance to anything we'd find in North Africa, I had gleaned that we might encounter similar soils to those of Burgundy, and the Rhône was the home of Syrah, the grape that made Gérard's Moroccan wine. I could use these as benchmarks for what we might encounter in Africa, and use a fleeting stop in Champagne to begin filming.

Having arrived in Champagne three hours earlier, we had by now expected to be on our way to Burgundy, our overnight stop, but so far little had gone to plan.

As we had crested a hill and seen our first vines, the view prompted us to start filming. A piece to camera, with the pretty town of Ay nestling amongst the vineyards below, would be the perfect way to prepare for the celluloid masterpiece that would hopefully win us a shower of accolades at film festivals. All we needed was a minute's introduction capped by the link: 'Now let's go down for a glass!'

It had started well. We unpacked the equipment and set up by the roadside; and had that been the limit of our expectations, then you could say we did a good job. Philip pointed the camera at me and waited for me to begin.

'Bugger!'

I suspected that this might not be recommended as an opening line in my, as yet unread, 'how to film a documentary' guide, so I went for it again.

'Well here we are ... bugger, that's lame.'

The guide might consider the first words a start, but would probably conclude I had a point with the rest. I considered that maybe the professionals prepared some sort of script before speaking. The cheats! I felt I could now write an exposé on how presenters were not as off-the-cuff as they appeared. 'Give me five minutes and I'll write something out', I said to Philip. I'd thought that having been unscripted in front of audiences for years would prepare me for filming, though, as I wrote my first words, the realisation that this was an entirely different genre began to unnerve me.

'Focus,' I thought, we only need a minute of footage after all.

After half an hour I had a few lines that I felt might do. I timed how long it would take me to say them. Twenty seconds! 'Bugger!'

When, an hour later, I finally uttered the words: 'Now let's go down for a glass,' I hoped that my genuine desire for alcohol might come across as simple enthusiasm.

I had chosen the village of Ay as it is home to Bollinger. I had worked for a distributor of theirs in the nineties and had visited Clos Saint-Jacques, a vineyard responsible for Vieilles Vignes Francaises: Bollinger's best wine and in my opinion, Champagne's finest. The wine, quite distinct from most top champagnes, is utterly remarkable in character, having a seemingly endless array of aromatics that alter kaleidoscopically on the palate. This, and the fact that so little is produced, gives it a hefty price tag, so it wouldn't be an experience I'd be repeating at my own expense. I hoped that we could buy something at the cheaper end of their range and do a little filming next to the vineyard.

'You'll need to buy it in Reims sir,' said the lady behind Bollinger's guest reception. Twenty miles in the direction we'd come seemed counter-productive so I asked if there was anywhere closer.

'There is somewhere in Epernay.' Only two miles away.

'Excellent.'

'But being Monday, it's closed.'

'Couldn't I buy a glass from you?' I said, eying the ice bucket and glasses behind her.

'We do serve a glass as part of our tour sir.'

'Wonderful, can I get one of those?'

'Only on the tour, sir.'

'Great, when's the next tour?' I would wait until I got a glass and make a break for it.

'Tomorrow at ten sir.'

I declined translating the word 'bugger' and decided we would have to find a substitute bottle for the filming. There were at least ten other producers in the village; we would try one of those. It transpired that Bollinger was the only champagne house that didn't sell directly to the public. Perversely though, it was the only one open on a Monday. Two bars and a supermarket later, all closed, I was in the store, the object of my quest nearly within grasp.

I bought the bottle and a quick dash saw me installed back at the vineyard and enthusing about my tasting experience some years before. I omitted describing this tasting experience however: feeling that the stale sherry and rancid almond flavour of the old cava I'd bought might possibly detract from the piece.

Although this wasn't supposed to be one of those time-pressured scenarios that are the delight of reality TV programmes, we were now half a day into our schedule and it seemed we were behind by almost as much. There was only one ferry a week to Tunisia and if we missed it, half of the trip's appointments would be lost. This was a predicament compounded by our satellite navigation system (whom we'd christened Barbarella on account of her ability to make us act unquestioningly on her every command). Although devoid of emotion, she certainly had a keen sense of irony as she sent us the wrong way on the motorway and back to Reims. As we doubled back on the outskirts of the city, a stop at the services re-introduced me to the delights of the hole-in-the-ground loo. I can only imagine these are the result of a porcelain shortage in the seventies. Scruples don't normally stop me using the disabled loo when I encounter these medieval monstrosities, though as this was occupied I had no choice. As I struggled to keep my trailing clothing away from the target area, an ageing crooner on the tannoy warbled: *'Oui, c'est difficile, mais je t'aime.'* I agreed with the first sentiment, but having never been a fan of Johnny Halliday the consolation did nothing to lighten my mood. I held my head in my hands and wondered if this was how Alan Whicker started.

* * *

Some hours later we pulled off the motorway south of Dijon and took the back roads through Burgundy. The last of the evening sun was disappearing behind the sloping ridge above the vineyards, leaving the top of the ridge lit, with the sweep of vines below in darkness. There'd be no filming tonight, but, having all but decided to forget a career in presenting, and focus on drinking more instead, this came as a relief. Thoughts now turned to where we were to stay, what to eat, and more importantly how to replace the cava with something more palatable. Our failure to acquire a glass of champagne in Champagne did not bode well for accomplishing our tasks, though, as we drove among the vines with our windows down, these concerns momentarily receded. The day's warmth had encouraged the vines, the red soil, and even, it seemed, the limestone walls to give up their aromas and bring the place alive. These simple smells lent our experience a dimension every bit as penetrating as sight and sound.

The neatly trimmed rows of vines, no doubt earlier buzzing with the activities of ploughing, weeding and spraying, were now quiet, the workers having left for their homes in one of the villages dotted along the slope. I slowed the car to pick out the vineyard names as we passed. It was akin to driving along the spine of one of the world's greatest wine lists: Chambertin, Morey St Denis and

17

Musigny – all names of wines I was familiar with from tastings, though could rarely afford to drink.

The trip so far had taught me that expectation was something else I could not afford, so it was pleasantly exceeded when we saw a sign for a campsite. We followed a track through the vines to a stone-built farmhouse. As we approached the gate a ruddy-faced woman strode out of the door. The Alsatian on a chain gave her an unwelcoming air. She opened the gate with a scowl, though it seemed that this was just the way that God had arranged her face, and she was perfectly charming when she spoke. We still gave the dog, whose opinion of us was unambiguous, a wide berth as she led us to where we could set up camp. The grassy patch granted us a view of the vineyards and the town of Nuits-Saint-Georges in the half-light. It was the perfect setting for us to unfold our new accommodation for the first time.

Now that sleeping arrangements were accounted for, we had our stomachs to tend to. On asking where we might find somewhere to eat, she drew a breath and said that there were restaurants in Nuits-Saint-Georges, but they were expensive. We were undeterred – the day had left us in need of celebration (though of what, if asked, I couldn't answer). Noticing that the tent was on the roof of the car, she said the farm gates were locked at ten, so we'd be locked out if we drove and we'd need to drive to make last orders. We had the option of driving our car and tent to a restaurant, but having nowhere to sleep, or having somewhere to sleep, but no food. Our shoulders dropped. We decided that we would rather have somewhere to sleep.

Seeing our resignation, she clapped a hand on Philip's arm and asked whether she could make something to eat for us. Our near ecstatic response brought a smile to her face and she said that she had some mussels, snails and steak she could prepare. When she said that the vines beside the property were also hers, and would we like red or white wine to accompany the food, we wanted to hug her, but the dog eyed us deteringly.

As we opened up the tent and set our table, Philip suggested that the timings given by our host might have been manufactured in her favour, as there was a price for the food and wine. We decided that it was better to count our blessings and enjoy the moment. This is a sentiment we also applied to the wine as we ate our meal. Whilst I wouldn't want to indulge it with a tasting note, it was gratefully received. Place and state of mind play a large part in a wine's appreciation. Ask anyone who's brought a bottle back from holiday and thought it didn't travel. What does not travel is the setting you are in and your state of mind. The wine is the same.

Totally replete, we left the debris to the night and clambered into the tent, sleeping so soundly that we were only woken by the TGV passing on the other side of the hedge, long after my poorly set alarm should have gone off.

When planning the trip I had decided to schedule a visit whilst passing through Burgundy, as I had found out that some of the North African vineyards would have similar soils. Having been to Burgundy a number of times before, I wanted to meet with a producer I hadn't visited, and, there being time for only one slot, it had to be the best.

Domaine de la Romanée-Conti is peerless in Burgundy. The estate's flagship wine, Romanée-Conti, sits a full head and shoulders above the competition, and, being Burgundy, that's stiff competition. In short, it is considered by many to be the world's finest red and regularly trades as such, vying only with Château Petrus in Bordeaux for top spot. Suspecting a visit would not be easy to come by, I worked the phone to pull in some favours and gained an introduction to their agent in the UK. I made the call. The contact, a man whose articulation made the Queen sound as if she came from a sink estate, asked me to e-mail a formal request for a visit. The reply was quick. In fact so swift as to leave me doubting whether the request had been made to the vineyard at all. I suppose it didn't take him long to consider their probable reaction to a request for a visit by a writer unknown to them coming with a tent. He politely explained that the estate receives many such requests, and they can only accommodate their most important clients. I hesitated before countering that I had recently spent nearly two thousand pounds on their wine for a tasting, though supposed that 'most important' wouldn't include purchasers of a single bottle.

I had scheduled a morning's filming amongst the vines instead, making the lateness of our awakening less of a drama. In fact we had a full four hours before we needed to rejoin the motorway and head south for the Rhône. We could no doubt get something 'in the can' in plenty of time.

As our host was already off tending her vines we deposited our payment cautiously into a box on the wall next to the dog's kennel and set off for the village of Vosne Romanée, the home of Domaine de la Romanée-Conti. Whilst Philip had persuaded me not to doorstep the owners, I wanted to visit the vineyard and see the soil. Normally mud doesn't do much for me, but when you stop to consider that it's directly responsible for the flavours in your glass, it gets a bit more interesting. Nobody can explain exactly why two plots next to one another, planted with the same vines and made in the same way, will taste differently. In Burgundy a few metres can mean the difference between ten pounds and a thousand pounds a bottle.

After a croissant, espresso and a few passive lungfuls of Gauloises in the village square, we again went in search of a bottle with which to film. Keeping an eye on time, we plumped for the first producer we came across. We bought a bottle of Gevrey-Chambertin and split up: Philip would get some mood shots in the area, whilst I would prepare a script. I had my notepad, the bottle and a corkscrew. Simple tools, but sometimes, like oil and water, they don't best mix.

I looked to the top of the ridge above the vineyards; the perfect spot to be inspired, I thought. On my way up I stopped next to the low wall surrounding the Romanée-Conti vineyard and snapped a few shots of the limestone-studded, firebrick-coloured earth (if there was soil pornography, this would be the centrefold), then made my way to the top. When I arrived I knew that if I couldn't be inspired here, then I should give up entirely. To say a sea of vines spread down the hill before me might be clichéd, but there's no better way of describing the sight of workers immersed chest-down in a swathe of green, their parked vans only half visible.

I stood beneath the shade of a large oak and poured myself a glass. Some way below I saw Philip filming in the heat of the morning and knew I had taken the cushy option here. However, as I nosed the wine I was forced to reconsider. We'd paid twenty-five euros for the bottle, but the contents weren't worth four! I had ignored the key rule in Burgundy: go with a producer you know, or taste it first. Because many producers make wine from the same vineyard, a lot of highly priced Burgundy is a con; you often pay for the vineyard name on the label, rather than the quality in bottle. But this didn't stop me drinking the stuff as I tried to grind out something to say. A woman who had been pruning nearby approached me as I did. Concerned at seeing a man pacing about whilst talking to himself and drinking, she had come to see if I needed help. She left, still unconvinced that I didn't. A passing couple also stopped me and asked if I knew where Romanée-Conti was. I pointed

21

them towards the vineyard. As they made their way down I saw a minibus draw up with a tour group next to the vineyard. They joined a couple of cyclists reading the brass tablet on the wall announcing that they had found their holy grail. I sat down under the tree and watched as people came and went, all respecting the sign's request that the vineyard be left untrodden. Here was a small piece of land responsible for millions of pounds worth of wine a year, protected by the world's most polite 'Keep Out!' sign. Those at the entrance to the smallest pieces of woodland back at home warn of dogs, shotgun or even legal action (on the Surrey side of the Sussex border anyhow). It seems that respect garners respect. I vaguely remember thinking that I ought to jot down something along these lines when I felt my eyelids overcome by gravity.

The honking of a horn stirred my consciousness. At first it was the foghorn of a bottle-shaped lighthouse above a sea of vines on which white vans were sailing (I blame the Gevrey-Chambertin), though its familiarity soon caused me to open my eyes. Before me, sporting a weighty camera and the glow of hard work, stood a frowning South African.

'I can explain,' I said. 'I have drunk a nasty bottle of wine and written nothing of value.' Fair explanation I thought, though his looks suggested I would have been better off lying. We filmed a piece with a little wine-induced confidence that I hoped might disguise its lack of preparation, and packed up. As we did, Philip offered to drive, though I detected something in his tone that hinted at sarcasm. It hit home when he asked if sir would care to recline in the back as we pulled away, though not until after I had already done so.

* * *

As the opaque purple liquid splashed into our glasses and I took my first sniff of Syrah, I wondered whether I had made a mistake in organising a visit in the Rhône. Maybe we should have just driven on.

We had arrived the night before and set up camp next to the river on the outskirts of Tain l'Hermitage, beneath the slope of the Hermitage hill. The term 'slope' belies the steepness of this vine-clad escarpment: in parts, 'gentle cliff' would better describe the home of one of France's most famous wines. The casual observer might wonder why anyone would ever bother to cultivate such a place, though one only needs to see the sunlight hitting the hill first thing in the morning, and last thing at night – before and after anywhere else around – to know why. It simply gets more sun than other vineyards, and that's a good thing for the Syrah here. It's the only red grape grown on the hill and there's still no finer example of its wine than that which is drawn from this chunk of granite. I was keen to taste the world's best Syrah as a benchmark because it's the grape at the heart of Gérard Depardieu's wine, the one that had set us on our quest.

When a friend working for an importer had helped me organise a visit to Maison Chapoutier, one of the hill's top winemakers, he had added a footnote to their reply. The e-mail had asked whether I'd like to conduct a vertical tasting (that's a range of years, not whether I'd be able to stand up) of their best Hermitage on the hill itself. Not too cryptically he had added: 'Does a bear …?'

I concurred. If you were going to have a benchmark, this was about as good as it gets. Whilst not commanding the same prices, their vineyard is just about what Romanée-Conti is to Burgundy – the jewel in the crown of a great region.

The visit had gone well so far. We were with Gregory,

Chapoutier's charismatic vineyard manager, and Bruno, their passionate winemaker. They had led us around various plots on the hill, enthusiastically explaining the differences. Initially busy with his camera, after an hour or so Philip had put the setting to autopilot and began texting a friend. (Poor boy! He'd yet to be converted to the pleasures of sifting topsoil though his fingers, squeezing the firm but yielding skin of a ripening grape, gripping the ... sorry, where was I?) We had reached the little chapel at the summit that gives rise to the name Hermitage and were enjoying the view as Bruno began to open bottles. Caught on the wind, sounds from the river could occasionally be heard: freighters, barges and lesser vessels using the channel for livelihood or pleasure. The signs of large industry dotted along the bank further south were at odds with the butterflies flitting about the carthorse working the vines next to us. Gregory explained that everything was done in tune with nature in the vineyard to encourage a harmonious balance. The horse provided the fertiliser, and the herbicides and pesticides were made from natural plant infusions. I asked if that made a difference to flavour and candidly he said probably not, but it was still better for the health of the vineyard and those drinking the wines if there weren't chemicals used. He said their vines were cultivated biodynamically, which is like a holistic, turbocharged form of organic, where processes in the vineyard and winery are done in tune with the cosmos. When I asked whether that affected flavour he said I'd have to ask his boss, Mr Chapoutier, as 'that's his thing'. To say I detected a note of scepticism would be unfair, though the complexities of this practice are often only fully understood by the true believers.

Whether it was due to spirituality or not, I knew something was working here as we tasted the wines. They were, without exception, classics. In the UK I'd been asked,

'Why bother tasting Hermitage, when nothing in Africa can live up to it?' and had then wondered whether I wasn't setting my sights too high. My smile afterwards was not just because I had tasted some fabulous wines. It was more down to a realisation that there was something about the wine in the TV studio that told me North Africa had the potential to make wine every bit as good.

* * *

Heading south through Provence brought with it an increase in temperature and a real sense that we were now only one stop from Africa's doorstep. The car's adjustable air conditioning (windows) allowed the resinous aromas of oak, thyme and lavender to fill the cabin as we drove. The sky seemed bluer and even the music was improving to my ears, but I still lessened the volume on Barry White as we passed through towns.

On arrival in the hills above Marseilles we quickly found 'le camping' and followed a narrow lane between two rows of pines to a high gate. The gate's razor wire and peeling paint suggested we had found somewhere intentionally overlooked by the Michelin guide. We thought to leave, though being in a car with a turning circle only marginally tighter than an oil freighter's, we rang the bell. The gate slid back and a man in a football top stood wiping something from the ledge provided by his stomach. Seeing only empty plots punctuating the dense forest behind him, we asked if there was a sea view so we could make our excuses and leave.

'Go to number 14, you can see the sea from there,' was his reply. We drove over to the plot. Whilst a slither of azure could be seen through the trees, it was on a slope whose steepness would engender a degree of involuntary intimacy neither of us was happy with, so we decided to leave.

'Ca va?' The man, more agile than I had given him credit for, had materialised at the side of the car. The gate had now closed behind him.

'Oui,' I replied. Philip, not for the first time, looked exasperated at my misplaced sense of politeness, something he puts down to being English. I paid the man and said we needed to go into town to get some food. As the gate opened and let us through, Philip questioned why I would possibly want to stay there. I said that it was all part of my plan – we were not going back! He said that he was travelling with the only person he had known to commit a pay and run.

As we looked for somewhere else I received a text message from Gérard's agent in Italy.

'He knows you are trying to contact him,' read the screen. It seemed we were making headway! But, as the message contained no other information, I was unsure in which direction.

Having found another campsite for the night we had risen early to be in time for the weekly ferry to Tunis. My timekeeping also was something that was on the verge of becoming irritatingly English to Philip. Our ticket had recommended a 5am arrival for a noon crossing, so just to be sure we arrived at 4am. As we drove into the vast hangar I felt a little vindicated to see that we weren't the first waiting to board. The holding area was animated with all sorts of life: queues of foot passengers, flat-bed trucks brimming with goods (and the occasional worker on top), as well as the odd tourist car; but mostly there were vehicles with roofs piled high with the baggage of people on the move. Many of the bourgeoning stacks were covered with regulation blue plastic sheeting. It was at this point that we encountered our first instance of discrimination. Two uniformed customs officers were working up the line ahead of us, forcing the owners of vehicles without the blue covering to unpack everything down to toiletries, then re-pack, and in some cases to join the back of the queue. The manner of their thoroughness suggested it could be a long morning. We began to think how we would best explain the security gear, camera equipment and laptops when they simply smiled and passed us by: they were only interested in the Tunisian registered vehicles.

At the far end of the hangar stood a stall surrounded by men smoking water-filled hookah pipes. The coffee it sold, strong enough to penetrate their sweet tobacco smoke, was like a siren call. As we made our way over I took the opportunity to use the loo and in doing so committed my first Muslim faux pas. On entering the cubicle with its now familiar hole, I discovered there was no lock. I placed my foot against the door and contorted myself in what must have looked like an unsavoury form of the game Twister. My mother had taught me to whistle in such circumstances, so what more appropriate than the Marseillaise to ward off potential embarrassment. I discovered that I didn't know much more than the opening bar, so, having repeated it with some gusto five or six times, I moved on to 'God Save the Queen', 'Land of Hope and Glory' and 'I Can Feel It Coming In The Air Tonight' by Phil Collins (the CDs were getting to me). The last rendition tailed off rather abruptly as I opened the door to a queue of women in hijab dress. I looked back at the door and momentarily thought of pointing out the similarity between the ladies and gents silhouettes on the signs but decided not to add further insult.

Once on board, the throng of humanity dispersed throughout the vessel, which, possibly a seasoned campaigner from other routes, seemed larger than necessary. We sat by the pool, which we had to ourselves. Should we wish to take the plunge, the cargo netting strung six feet above the inch of trapped sea-spray would break our fall. Philip made a call to activate his mobile broadband in Africa. So far he had incurred the same bill on the trip that I would in a year, and each time he used the phone it made me question whether I should get more friends.

I started to jot down a few ideas for filming later, though the stress Philip was experiencing in conversing with his provider was becoming osmotic, so I decided to wander off in search of something to eat.

There were three restaurants on board: all closed – presumably managed by someone who had attended catering school in Champagne. The duty free offered bars of nougat, along with vodka and cigarettes. The first two options were so shrouded in dust that they were camouflaged against the brown wallpaper; and the other was so popular it required a member of staff just to re-stock the shelf. The shop assistant told me I could get nutella pancakes from a griddle in the bar. This did not bode well for the twenty-four hour crossing, though it did explain why crewmembers were either stick thin or obese – I made a mental note to smuggle a little fruit on for them when we returned. I arrived in the bar and spotted a bottle of Tunisian wine on the shelf. I bought it, though the purchase was an infrequent one, as the barman said that he didn't have a bottle opener and would I mind coming back later. Ever prepared, I offered him mine. I could sense his concern for my creed as he opened it up.

I wondered whether the ideal match for the wine would be a silky reduction of cocoa and praline in a fine pastry timbale, so ordered a couple of nutella pancakes.

Back at the poolside I found Philip gone and in his place were thirty men watching football on a portable television.

They weren't the usual football crowd. Almost contemplative, they watched and passed comment to one another in an easy fashion. I had also found where the cigarettes were ending up. The television had been put on a low table, no doubt to be visible below the grey haze that hung heavy in the air. I scoured the ship but found every area with a similar scene; apparently Tunisia was playing Morocco in the African Nations Cup. I noticed some fans stop watching at one point to pray. As Tunisia was already winning, this was likely due to spiritual routine rather than specifically for the team.

I saw another European face and gave a cheery hello. The man reacted as if we were passing each other in Guildford, and simply ignored me. It struck me that I had said hello because we were in the minority. Maybe the man was more comfortable standing out in a crowd; or maybe he was just from Guildford.

I eventually found Philip on deck, still in conversation with an operative from the phone company. The call was cut short seconds later after we left European waters, the company having torn up their agreement with their African partners – something that very nearly sent the space-aged handset into orbit. I consoled him with a glass of Tunisian Syrah and a pancake. He smiled as he took a sip, uttering something about red fruit jam and spice. The wine, one eighth the price and three times the quality of the Gevrey-Chambertin, reassured me that the premise of the trip had been well founded.

Into Africa – Tunisia

The feeling of having arrived was complete as we drove between the twin peaks east of Tunis. The urban landscape had given way to a colourful patchwork of fruit groves, olive trees and scrub, the low valley signalling an end to industrialisation as if holding the commercial centre back. The sweet scent of pink and white oleander lining the carriageway mixed with fig, usurping the acrid smell of burnt tyre and concrete dust of the suburbs, which, like most, had revealed little of the nation's true culture.

A vaudeville-like registration process, involving form filling and document stamping at the offices of five morbidly disinterested clerks, had preceded our release into the country. Devoid of satellite navigation, we'd stopped beyond the entry gates to plan our route to Korba – a village on the east coast of Cap Bon, the wide peninsula jutting into the Mediterranean. After a bit of digging around in the back, a quick call confirmed that we hadn't lost our maps and travel guides for the tour after all – they were still on my desk in Haslemere. There was nothing for it. We would have to go straight to the last resort of a man and ask for directions! Having no guides meant knowing nothing about the areas that we were travelling through. Again, we would have to talk to people instead of relying on the thoughts of a travel writer in Battersea: not such a bad thing as it turned out.

As we journeyed east we realised maps were only

necessary for countries in which people didn't have any time for you. We quickly found that the fixed enquiring faces of those we approached would break into a broad grin when they themselves were greeted with a smile. We found that most spoke French, as well as their native Arabic, and whilst not all of the directions may have pleased Barbarella (she was a control freak), we arrived with time to spare before our first visit.

We found our pre-arranged meeting spot, a little bar at Korba's crossroads, and ordered a plate of fried prawns, calamari and bread; all items I was confident should not lead to gastro-rejection by our pampered western stomachs. I waved away some salad garnish as it arrived and plucked the ice cubes from our drinks, much to the amusement of the barman, and to Philip's surprise.

'Aren't you being a little anally retentive?'

'Yes, and I intend to remain so,' I quipped.

As Philip re-called the salad, I flashed him the 'ignore me at your peril' stare.

Our contact appeared a little after the expected time from behind a large set of gates next to the bar. He was an elegant bespectacled man with silver hair and a pronounced limp, wearing neatly pressed chino trousers and an expensive safari jacket – not what I had expected. When Didier, his associate with whom I'd made the appointment, had described Rached as his Tunisian colleague, I had expected someone … well, more Tunisian. He seemed a little surprised at seeing us at the bar, explaining that we should have come to the gate: 'it was better for our security'. This unnerved me a little, though I put it down to a difference in understanding (my French being tested for the first time in a while). I'd checked Tunisian politics and the country wasn't having the same problems as Algeria. So far, we felt safer here than we might in many parts of the UK.

Introductions over, he went to fetch his car from behind the gates and told us to follow him to the winery. He led us a little way out of town and turned off between two patches of cacti at the roadside. The deeply pitted earth in front of us, barely a track at all, gave us our first off-road experience in Africa – somewhat diminished by the sight of the gleaming black vintage Mercedes we were following. Three children stopped playing football and chased our car for a short way. Women sieving couscous looked up, then returned to their work as oxen laboured beside them in the fields. I considered that, as winery driveways go, this was rudimentary but it lost nothing for it. The modest drive didn't prepare us for the winery itself however. The juxtaposition between it and the four-storey ochre building modelled on a Carthaginian castle couldn't have been more striking. The flat roof and rounded ramparts were classically Tunisian, though the warm pastel colours were Moroccan. The uniform white of the buildings we'd so far seen would make a Tunisian paint salesman's job a tedious one.

The inside was as impressive as outside, and had clearly been built with high quality wine in mind. An elegant tasting area in mottled coral pink gave way to a cavernous hall housing gleaming new tanks; veterans of only three harvests. A phalanx of pupitres (the wooden sandwich-board racks used to make champagne) bristled with bottles; the yeast deposits slowly slipping towards the bottle caps would be removed in a week or two. I began to ask a few winemaking questions, but was told that Didier was the best man to answer these. I asked when we would get to meet him.

'It would be easier to e-mail him, he is in France.'

On asking if we could see the barrel cellar, I was handed a brochure. Our host did not have keys. This was not going well. I hesitated before asking what Rached did for the winery in fear of appearing exasperated. I supposed that he was on the vine-growing side of the business and asked if we could see the vineyards. He led us out of the winery and pointed to the crest of a sweeping hill behind the building.

'There they are. I shall wait for you here,' he said, tapping his bad leg.

Even the quality of the soil, a milky coffee colour thick with pebbles (I was a little excited, I admit it) didn't make up for the fact that I'd be finding out nothing more about the vines either until back home. I consoled myself as I walked back down that the trip was about the wines, and, judging by the vineyards and the equipment, they should be good.

The sight of Rached standing by his car however, having locked the winery, did not suggest that we would be finding out. Philip looked at me consolingly. He knew that this was one of my best hopes of finding great wine in Tunisia and could sense my frustration.

'I'll lead you back,' our host called. With hindsight, I'm glad I wasn't given the opportunity to say anything before we got into our car, as it might not have been diplomatic enough. He had, after all, been generous with his time, and I could easily not have got to see the property at all.

Back in Korba, we drew up at the bar in order to stop and thank Rachid, but he drove directly to the security gates he'd emerged from. We followed. A guard scuttled from his post and swung the gates open without word, taking his hat off as he allowed Rached's car past. I slowed, though the guard simply waved us on with a nod.

Nothing could have been further removed from the town's plain buildings and dusty streets than the scene beyond the gates. A smoothly paved avenue snaked between individually designed cottages, the gardens of which brimmed with bougainvillea, roses and other flowers, whose combined colour made us realise how little of it there was outside. The sheen of fruit-laden date palms and the uniform health of the plants throughout indicated a level of attention given by professionals rather than the residents. Three white-coated staff crossed our path carrying towels, flowers and a massage table; but it was otherwise deserted. A little way in, the avenue widened into a square, the focus of which was a magnificent terracotta dome flanked by smaller pillared buildings. Rached beckoned us in and on past a reception desk, the staff of which seemed to stiffen a little as he acknowledged them. Parakeets flew amongst the creepers trailing from the brightly painted ceiling high above. He led us down a long vaulted gallery at the end of which the Mediterranean could be seen. I was about to ask where we were going, when a large man stepped from between two pillars and clasped a hand on Rached's shoulder. He laughed and said, 'Everything is ready' before leaving us again. We reached a white beach. A wooden bridge led to a tiny shaded island, large enough for a table and chairs. We crossed and were invited to sit. Pleasantly bemused, we watched as the man we'd seen moments earlier reappeared with two splendidly uniformed waiters. Between them they held a large bowl of orange lilies. One of the waiters plunged his arm among the flowers and pulled out a dripping bottle, then proceeded to open it. He announced the wine with a reverence heightened, we guessed, by the presence of Rached. When tasting wine I try not to let environment influence my opinion. Although I tried to ignore the gentle lapping waves on the deserted beach and the cry of macaw announcing that I was about to conduct a tasting in paradise, I was concerned that an element of partiality might creep into my tasting note:

K de Kurubis
Chardonnay. Méthode Traditionelle.
A mousse of tiny bubbles ripple across the palate like the last wave of a still summer's evening, caressing the tastebuds akin to the gentlest masseuse on supple flesh ...

I suspected I might have to taste the wine again under different conditions for the fact file. Thus we tasted all of the estate's wines; each new foray punctuated by delicate canapés and announced with equal formality by our sommelier. Although I had not spat all I'd tasted, I thought I should still be under the limit for driving. It was only then I considered that a Muslim country would no doubt have different restrictions. I asked Rached what the drink-drive limit was in Tunisia. He looked wryly at me.

'How much can you drink before you cannot drive?'

Apparently, although around thirty per cent of the Muslim population consume alcohol (I could find no official figures, though this was the average quoted), there are no drink-drive laws. There might just be one governing not hitting other people with your car however, so I declined a full glass when offered. Rached looked surprised. I explained that I didn't know how far we'd need to drive to find a campsite. Either there are no campsites in Tunisia, or camping was alien to him, as it took a while to explain the concept. He seemed intrigued and offered to try and find one should we wish to stay at such a place rather than here at the club as his guest. Needless to say, we instantly adjusted our plans.

When pressed, Rached, clearly a modest man, explained that the wine estate was his, along with, it seemed, a fair amount of Korba. His major business interests included strawberry and tomato processing, and he had been the town's mayor at one stage. He explained that he didn't normally involve himself in the day to day running of the winery, though he had agreed to a request to meet us from Didier, who was out of the country. There is probably some sort of moral attached to this tale, concerning judgements made on first impressions, though I don't wish to find it, as it will make me look a bit of a tit.

After Rached had bid us goodnight, Philip and I sat with the remnants of a fire-roasted chicken and the bottles from the tasting. The quality of the wines seemed to further improve. Whether this was because they'd had a chance to breathe, or due to their marriage with the food, or even because of the setting, I couldn't say; though as we began a game of boules in the warm Mediterranean breeze that carried the scent of turmeric and beach cacti, I wasn't too bothered.

* * *

Because I am someone who questions the pained look on a jogger's face with wonder, it took Philip a little while to convince me that a run along the beach would be the perfect tonic for the morning's woolliness. In the same way that you shouldn't leave food on a plate, we had decided not to insult our host by leaving the bottles unfinished. As I bounced along – a puppet on steroids, I think Philip said – I thought about the wines we'd tasted. They'd been a great start and would shame many at three times the price in supermarkets in the UK. I considered whether, given time, the winery had the potential to compete at the very highest level; after all, the vines were young and the property had just started out.

As we passed a fisherman gathering his net from the sea, I wondered what our appointment later that morning might bring. We waved at the man examining his empty haul but he turned away. Perhaps he had considered the perversity of the situation where we were in pursuit of calorie-loss, and he was expending them unsuccessfully merely to survive. Or maybe he was just appalled at my running technique.

'This is magnifique,' declared Samia as she passed me a glass of inky purple liquid.

My normal reaction to such a statement is to look for the contrary viewpoint, but I knew that I'd need to gather my nerve before challenging her. If my first visit hadn't taught me to dispense with preconceptions, then the opening moments of my second would certainly have done so.

We had left our little oasis and travelled to Domaine Neferis, an estate nestled in a mountainous amphitheatre halfway back to Tunis. The vast curve created by the surrounding ridge channels cool air from the sea, assisting the cultivation of more than just vines. Much of the land within the basin was swathed in citrus, nut and olive plantations. The estate's villa, with its warm sandstone walls and red clay tiles, looked to have been plucked from a Tuscan landscape, the cypresses in the drive suggesting this was the intention. The figure coming down the villa steps gave the theme further impact; the large dark sunglasses and neat denim were those of an Italian starlet – not at all what I had expected.

My knowledge of Muslim society prior to arrival was scant, and, where women were concerned, I had expected Tunisia to conform to the stereotypical image of an Islamic state. This is something that Samia, our host, a female Muslim winemaker (not necessarily in that order), was presumably aware of as she began explaining that Tunisia is highly progressive in matters regarding women's rights. These rights were enshrined in law by Habib Bourguiba, the country's first president after Independence in 1956. Known by some as the 'liberator of women', he banned polygamy as

37

well as the wearing of the hijab in schools. His actions were not, as you might expect, roundly supported by all and there are still many men who consider giving such rights to women a dangerous thing – dangerous for the women of course! As we toured the winery, this was something I sensed from one or two of the junior male workers. Whilst they accorded her respect, they felt they had to make light of the fact that they were taking orders from a woman and joked about it; something she was able to take in her stride and handle with humour to her benefit. She also explained that only women were employed to pick in the vineyards because she required a rigorous selection of grapes, and men tended to lose focus a little too easily.

I was beginning to think that any piece of writing on the winery would be a shoe-in on *Woman's Hour*, when a glance along the rows in one vineyard suggested a letter to Germaine Greer might be more appropriate. A leftover from colonial times, these old vines were in the traditional 'bush' form. The short branches on each vine reached no more than three feet above the ground, meaning that the grapes would have to be picked at about half that height (back-wrenching work that would have the Health and Safety Executive in the UK spluttering into their Horlicks). If anyone tried to pull up these vines though, they would be losing something special. These gnarled old plants with their thick twisting trunks provide the juice for arguably Tunisia's best wine, Selian Reserve. This argument I was about to have with Samia.

The vines are Carignan, normally as unwelcome a component in good wine as antifreeze. They are generally planted for reasons of quantity as they produce lots of fat sugary grapes, but these make flabby alcoholic wines. In North Africa Carignan was planted by the French, who wanted to beef up some of their acidic table wines at home.

38

After Independence, most of the plantings were ripped up, though some remained; and, as they aged, their wines began to improve.

Vines, in keeping with most organisms, become less vigorous with age. In youth they grow with abandon, producing shoots, leaves and branches without too much care for the quality of their output (typical adolescents); but as they mature, quality begins to outweigh quantity in their ambitions. To produce smaller more flavoursome berries becomes their aim and it's a canny one, as birds will go for these first, making vine reproduction more effective. In part, the reason for the improvement is that they take up less water as they lose vigour, so the juice is more concentrated. Also, the roots pass deeper through the earth with time, picking up different nutrients, which assists diversity of flavour.

So it was with some expectation that we entered the villa. There, a table lined with bottles awaited, one of which contained Selian Reserve, the product of these wizened old plants. Its reputation had me expecting it to be a contender for wine of the trip.

We had all but tasted through their excellent range and had only two wines left. Unusually, the best was not being saved until last. Beyond the object of my anticipation – the Selian Reserve, a sleek black bottle with an elegant gilt label – stood a plain one with a handwritten tag.

Samia poured the Selian Reserve, stating, without boast, that many considered it to be the finest wine in Tunisia. As I tasted I was in no mind to argue, because the wine was indeed excellent: vivid aromas reminiscent of fruit pastilles, oak smoke and chocolate were supported by a texture that coated the mouth like damson jelly. My disagreement only came when I tasted the wine in the plain bottle. I maintained the Selian Reserve couldn't be the best in my eyes, at least not when they were making a wine like the last one. She smiled and said that its quality was why they were going to call it Magnifique, showing us the writing on the tag.

As we drove to our afternoon meeting my mind was still preoccupied by the last wine, and a theme that seemed to be developing. Once again the grape responsible was Syrah; and, although the vines were still young, its aromatics were more diverse than the Selian Reserve; and the structure, whilst still powerful, more elegant. In short, it was more of a wine. If made with the same care year-on-year, the wine would only get better. Fabulous now, could this be a future great to compete with the world's best?

* * *

'There could be snakes – just stamp your feet and you'll be fine.'

The reassurance consoled Philip little as we pushed through the long grass – his phobia had him creating more vibration than the All Blacks performing the haka.

Having visited the winery and tasted the wines at our next meeting, Ludovic, our host, was taking us to something he was keen to show us.

We were half way through our visit at the new Ceptunes winery, in the hills above Grombalia. The air was cooler up here than on the valley floor at Domaine Neferis that morning. A breeze shepherded a column of smoke sideways on a nearby farm. Rounded stacks of hay reminiscent of a bygone age sat in a field some way below and olive trees dotted the slopes about us; but there were no vines. The banks of stainless steel tanks we had seen were big enough to accommodate juice from a sizeable estate, so I asked where the vineyards were. Ludovic explained they owned no vineyards, but bought grapes in from different growers for their wines. In the eyes of some this might be enough to engender a prejudiced view of their output, the thought being that they might have less control over aspects governing quality in the vineyard. However many good wines, including most champagnes, are made from bought grapes. There is also a fairly strong fiscal reason for not having your own vineyards in Tunisia – they could be taken away from you. Vineyard land is leased from the state, and, although there is the option of renewal, the more cautious might see this as enough reason to restrict long-term investment; not that it appeared lacking in any way at Ceptunes.

Ludovic proudly swung his arm back and asked us what we thought. I thought, 'It's a building site,' though didn't want to say and instead looked suitably impressed. What did strike me, though, was a potential business opportunity: someone could make a lot of money in Tunisia by starting a scaffolding company. What we saw made me suspect Heath Robinson was inspired by Tunisian builders, but even he could not match their imagination. Men with paintbrushes hung from ropes, wheelbarrows were being pushed across plank walkways that would petrify trapeze artists, and all manner of other improvised methods were employed to get workers up to where they were needed. This is not to say that their labours were haphazard, however. As we drew closer the craftsmanship was apparent. Fine mosaic tiles were being applied to the walls with the delicacy of a television chef balancing a chive on a canapé, and many contemporary artists would do well to emulate the skill of those applying gloss paint to the walls. Ludovic led us to an empty vaulted hall and encouraged us to envisage what would be Tunisia's first serious foray into wine tourism. This was to be a restaurant, and what was now a dusty concrete balcony, running the length of the hall above scrub and aggregate, would become a shaded tasting veranda overlooking palm groves and sunken gardens; the latter providing fresh produce for the kitchen. In time there would be concerts, art exhibitions and a boutique. This is nothing new to anyone who has visited California's Napa Valley, but in a society where wine is barely tolerated this is a bold statement indeed; a move that is doubtless needed if the world is going to take the country's wine seriously.

To our relief Ludovic was familiar with camping. He said that if we liked we could pitch at the winery, though with a look that suggested it wasn't something he would do himself. The lack of absolute conviction led us to ask if there was anywhere further afield. He said we could follow him to Hammamet, he was going there anyway and he'd heard of a place we might camp at. The town's name was familiar and we hoped it might provide a more engaging evening than a night in the scrub.

In less than half an hour we were back at the coast some way south of where we'd been the previous evening. We would have considered returning to the oasis, though having seen the normal tariff we decided to save the amount should the car break down – then we could fly first class between visits. Ludovic dropped us off by a set of gates similar to those from the night before. Thinking it might be out of our league we pressed the bell anyway and were promptly attended to by a man in a crisp white robe who appeared through a door in the gate. He explained that they did take in campers and the fee was fifteen dinars. This was cheap. We handed over the notes and he disappeared. The gates slid back. Their purpose, as with those from before, was to stop those outside from looking in, though in this instance to secure payment 'site unseen'. The campsite would best be described as a car park, because, well, it was one. The dusty plot, whose only occupants were two sleeping dogs, abutted a small hotel the man operated.

We decided to find the man and complain, when we realised we might have jumped the gun. To one side of the car park extended a lush walled area shaded by a gnarled olive tree. The flower baskets and plants trailing from the walls would give us a sense of being back at our oasis. This was more like it. We took down the little rope cordon, drove in and set up camp. A little later, as we prepared to walk into the town for dinner, I began to deploy the car's security measures in the manner of swat team. Philip went to get directions to a restaurant, reminding me to spot-weld the doors. When he returned he asked if we were 'fully locked down and good to go'. I told him to 'roger that' – meaning the American vernacular, of course.

The directions were simple. The man had said to hit the beach and go right until you get to the town. But simple doesn't always mean easy.

Dusk was setting in with the kind of wonderful sunset you don't bother snapping as you know it will look cheesy on a photo. The beach was deserted and little could be seen in either direction. After a mile we saw our first signs of life. Two fishermen, more successful than their counterpart that morning, were unhooking a bream from one of their rods. This fact they offered up with a smile when asked (possibly due to the fact that I was walking instead of jogging). A while later we passed a small group of young men sat around an unhealthy looking fire. I refrained from pointing out the impact of burning rubber tyres on the environment as they didn't seem to be as jolly as the fishermen. A little further on we saw a guard counting surfboards on a Club Med beach. When we approached to ask how far the town was, he reacted, in our opinion, with delusions of grandeur. I'm not sure how, 'Freeze you sons of bitches, turn around and get your asses out of here,' sounds in Arabic, but I'm sure it wasn't far off what he was saying, so we moved on. We felt we were getting closer as larger buildings began to line the beachfront, yet there were another two miles of exclusive casinos and private resorts before we reached the town proper.

It was now dark. In need of a little local knowledge, we approached a taxi waiting by the entrance to what must have been the medina – the original walled city. Lit from the base, the towering fortification was the complete incarnation of a giant sandcastle. We were pleased when the man agreed to a request for a tour of the medina, though it seemed my French had led to a misunderstanding: we drove around the perimeter in silence for half a mile before stopping on the other side next to another entrance. The confusion was soon cleared up and we were on our tour: alone and on foot. There was no motorised access. Whether this was to preserve the ancient structure, or that to take a car in would mean to disassemble it, we weren't sure, as the road through the arch quickly fragmented into a series of high-sided alleyways through which an obese donkey might struggle. Now deserted, there was little sign that the medina was more active by day. The immaculately clean cobbles and smooth whitewashed walls suggested the pride of those living behind the plain blue doors. We supposed we might have to find sustenance outside of the walls, though for the moment we were content to wander and absorb the peace.

The medina was all there had been to Hammamet until recently. Passing out beyond the three fortified gates you would have set foot in the desert, where, as we had seen, miles of development now lay. This has been sympathetically contained below tree level however, a restriction written into law, and has had little impact on the historical heart. Even sound from outside seemed not to pollute the labyrinth through which we walked, the three-metre thick outer walls still serving to protect its inhabitants. Something however began to pervade our senses. At first it was a whiff of wood smoke, which intensified to include some form of cooking. It had caught the air some distance away, carried along the passageways. Philip, now used to my olfactory idiosyncrasies, was happy to indulge me as I tried to follow the scent. Music could now be heard to accompany it, a little like the consulate's telephone lute music, though in this context, eerily pleasing. As we continued, tobacco and the musk of perfume joined the smoky scent of what I could now make out as grilled fish. These enticing aromas led us down a wide set of worn steps and into a sunken area abutted by the seaward walls of the medina.

Mistaking a black-tie party for fancy dress and arriving in bondage would have made us feel more appropriately attired than among the elegant society lounging in the kasbah: safari shorts and hiking boots not something that Armani do a line in. This apparel a waiter graciously overlooked and asked if we would like to smoke a hookah or have some food. Indicating the latter, we were taken through an area of reclining glitterati with their bubbling pipes, a cover scene one might see if *Vogue* and *Smokers Weekly* were ever to merge. He sat us down and pointed to their menu – a table of crushed ice piled high with two types of fish: large and not so large. Having an appetite, we selected two of the former and asked, rather hesitantly, if they had any wine. Where there had been no need for printed matter regarding the food, the card he drew from his belt was entirely necessary due to the selection on offer. The waiter – in fact a sommelier with a good knowledge of wine – began to make some suggestions to accompany the fish. I failed to catch its name though it was ugly – not that I consider any fish particularly attractive. We liked the idea of a Gris d'Hammamet and he set off to find a bottle.

Gris, or grey, is a fairly unappealing term to describe the colour of anything, let alone the delicate onion-skin hue of the style easily distinguishable from rosé in North Africa. I suppose it's better than calling it l'oignon d'Hammamet, however. The wine is made from red grapes by pressing them and leaving the skins (where all the colour comes from) with the clear juice for no more than a few hours so it picks up a little tint only. Thus rosés, and reds in turn, are made by leaving the juice with skins for longer.

The wine was fresher than I had anticipated and modern in style. I asked the sommelier his opinion of the producer: Les Vignerons de Carthage. State owned, they are by far the largest in Tunisia and we would be visiting them in two days' time. He was very enthusiastic, expanding on a forward-thinking attitude recently adopted by the government with regard to wine production. He gave me details of which wines particularly to look out for when we went there. We chatted for a while before I thought to offer him a glass. He seemed surprised and politely declined: 'I don't consume alcohol.' This we found was not unusual throughout our trip. There are many employed in activities connected with wine (in fact probably the majority, including those on the winemaking staff in wineries) who, whilst deriving a living from it, consider its consumption against their religion (others interpret the Koran differently). Still, if I worked in a newsagent I would have to sell *Golf Monthly*.

We had a little trouble getting a taxi back – something to do with going north of the medina after midnight – though we eventually persuaded one to take us to our car park. Observing the old adage, we tiptoed past the sleeping canines and climbed into the tent.

The night passed without incident. Well, for me at least. Philip had unfortunately forgotten about the dogs on a trip to the loo. Once awoken, they were keen on a little exercise and clearly thought Philip, a fit man, could provide it. They chased him about the car park for some time, daring him to reach the object of his excursion. Although silent (he's a noble friend), the pursuit didn't go unnoticed by the hotel owner and the dogs were called off. Philip began to form a sentence that would adequately convey his displeasure when the owner saw we were camping in his flower garden and displayed a fair amount of his own. Philip's powers of diplomacy were clearly on form that night, as I was allowed to sleep on.

* * *

'Why are you here sir?'

I briefly thought this time of answering the question existentially but considered it might lead to confusion, or, if understood, arrest. I responded the same way I had the previous times we'd been stopped by police, saying that we were restaurateurs writing about the country's food. Why I chose not to mention the wine connection, I'm not sure. I suppose I was keen not to offend. This elicited the same cheery response as it had before and we were waved on our way. There had been checkpoints at almost every major junction we had encountered so far, and the few times we'd been stopped it had been out of curiosity alone. We considered ourselves grateful, stopped or not, as their presence was partly for our benefit. Apart from an incident in 2002, where a suicide bomber killed twenty-one people at a synagogue in Jerba, Tunisia has had little trouble with Al-Qaeda. One of the reasons is put down to a strong police presence.

We were retracing our route inland and back towards the vineyards. As the land rose I knew we were climbing into the eastern slopes of the Atlas mountain range, spanning the three countries in our quest. I pictured Gérard tending his vines with a pair of secateurs and an ageing wheelbarrow fifteen hundred miles away in Morocco, where the same range receded to sea level. I imagined a scene from *Jean de Florette*: the actor plucking a leaf here, pulling a weed there, and hoped that his neighbours were more helpful than those in the film. Philip's look as I mentioned this indicated a certain level of concern for me, something he was unable to voice as we'd reached our destination. A bright red banner rippling between the pillars of the estate's entrance announced that we had arrived at Domaine Atlas. We felt a little foolish waiting by the vast iron gates whilst others drove through a wide gap in a hedge to one side, untroubled by the guard making his way from a sentry box.

When I had arranged our meeting I had been told that Imed, the winemaker, would be able to conduct a twenty-minute tour but would then have to attend to a group of tourists. Being a Sunday, we were delighted that he was happy to offer his time at all and I had planned some questions to cover quickly what I needed to know.

The guard opened the gate and motioned us in. We pulled up next to a straw-covered veranda in a dirt courtyard, which had at some stage been a horse corral. The modest white buildings surrounding us, and the cartwheels adorning the walls, made me wish I had packed a poncho and some cigars – I had an idea for our film. Philip pointed out that this had already been done.

A man in his mid-thirties wearing black jeans and black shirt warmly greeted us. His easy smile and relaxed manner marked him out as someone used to welcoming visitors, though his prolonged eye contact suggested that he was also used to calculating the amount of time he ought to spend with them. I asked my first question. Imed's considered response suggested that twenty minutes would be insufficient time for our visit. In answer to 'I understand you have a meeting with some tourists in twenty minutes', he had covered the economic, political and religious implications of being the only winery to sell directly to the public. It transpired that they only had an export licence, though as this included sales to non-nationals visiting the country, a fair amount of trade was conducted this way.

Before a second question could be posed, an aide came to his side and announced that their visitors had arrived. He looked apologetic and explained that he would have to tend to his guests though he'd be happy to continue later if we had time. In the meantime, he explained, we could spend a while by a lake in the mountains. This sounded idyllic, and having heard that wild brown trout were still to be found in the Atlas, I asked if we might take our fishing rod. He said he didn't see why not. It turned out that he was as unaware of Tunisian law as we were. He encouraged us to take the winery's guard as an escort, again for our safety. We tried to decline but he was insistent. Feeling a little mollycoddled, I motioned for the guard to follow us and drove off. A check in the rear view mirror a few hundred yards up the road confirmed that he was following. It also confirmed his commitment, as he was running. I pulled up and he jumped in clutching his chest in a disconcerting manner, and we drove on.

The mountain road thinned and turned to dirt track. Within ten minutes cacti and dry grass had given way to heather and pine trees. As we rounded a corner our escort encouraged me to slow down – more gates. This time they were abutted by chain link fence and razor wire. It appeared even the fish needed security here. Was everybody paranoid? Cameras in the trees covered the entrance and a sentry post suggested it was more than the trout being guarded. A door opened and a uniformed official approached. Monitor screens could be seen behind him. Our escort descended. Philip and I watched as the two guards conversed in a series of barks. This clearly was the way guards best communicate and the gates were quickly opened. We were asked to drive in and park up, we would be walking from there. Taking out our backpacks, we considered whether we should bring a bottle of wine, though decided that it might upset our escort. The official returned to his post and the three of us took a path through the trees. We soon came to a narrow shingle beach. The lake was more a small sea encircled by mountains. At one end a vast dam held the powder-blue water in place. The area was silent except for the lapping of waves on the shore.

I took off my backpack and set it on the ground before me, pulling out a small tin box, much to the intrigue of our escort. His interest continued as I pulled a length of nylon from the bag and tied it to the end of a thicker piece. The penny dropped as I drew out four short lengths of fishing rod and began to assemble them. Alarmed, he looked to the trees about us in near panic, shrilly explaining something in Arabic. I supposed he wasn't suggesting a Wickams Fancy would be the best fly to use in these waters and re-packed the rod, hoping to put him at ease. This began to have the desired effect until he turned and saw Philip setting up the camera. The heart attack we'd earlier averted was once again pending as he ran at Philip, waving his arms in a cutting motion like a frenzied Stephen Spielberg.

Suspecting that this might not be the spot to be getting some atmospheric shots of a fly line glistening in the sun, we agreed to our escort's suggestion that we return to the car. In fact 'suggestion' somewhat understates his intonation as he shepherded us back up the hill. A quick stop at the sentry post, accompanied by what looked to be some form of

50

impassioned plea, saw us on our way. He accepted our apologies as we drove back, which I felt began to smooth relations. A little later he also accepted a glass of wine from us, though I wasn't sure whether he normally drank wine or if our actions had driven him to put medicinal need before religion. A couple of days later, whilst travelling with the government, I casually asked a few questions regarding fishing and filming. We nodded with interest as we learnt that fishing is highly illegal on government waters and that filming in public places is only permissible with state written approval. Unsurprisingly, approval is never given for military installations, of which the lake was a part. So we'd scored a trifecta! I didn't ask about the penalties for such actions, for fear it would arouse suspicion. The guard gallantly said nothing when we returned to the winery. He walked back to his post no doubt hoping that in future he would be left to deal with less stressful duties such as fending off armed robbers.

Imed's guests had left and he had prepared a tasting in the winery for us. He led us into a new purpose-built structure behind the courtyard, full of shiny steel tanks and rows of new oak barrels. This was to be no usual tasting from bottle, but one from the barrels.

The first thing anyone needs to do when learning how to appreciate wine from barrel is to forget whether it tastes nice, because most of it doesn't: whites are often too sharp as the acidity hasn't softened, and reds too bitter because the tannins haven't mellowed. There's very little from barrel that you're going to enjoy, unless you're the sort that likes sucking on lemons or chewing headache tablets.

Not all good wines are aged in barrel. Many are not, though most wines that are tend to be of higher quality; that's because barrel ageing costs more, and only wines with character and potential can withstand ageing in oak – the wood tends to dominate otherwise. Good winemakers don't do it to add an oaky taste, but because it lends richness and allows the wine to breathe through the pores in the wood – the start of the wine's development. These tastings are all about detective work: putting everything together and trying to work out how the wine will age. The wine will also change when it is filtered and bottled, so this is not the sort of tasting that leaves you best informed about a winery's finished range.

So, that's the long way of saying that everything I tasted here was a little like sucking on lemons or chewing asprin – though saying that without the preamble might get me sued. There was good potential however. The wines, at this early stage of development, were packed with ripe fruity flavours and the star of the tasting once again was Syrah. Only time would tell how well Imed and his team would guide the developing wines into bottle.

As Imed led us from the tasting area and locked the winery up I offered him my card. He said that surely we'd be staying for lunch and that we could exchange details later. We were led back to the veranda where a large earthenware tajine and a bowl of cucumber salad sat on a table prepared for three. A dish of roasted sweet potatoes was brought out and hot tabouna, the traditional Berber bread, was sliced before us. He explained that it was the Muslim way – he felt it would be an insult to let us leave without eating. As he poured us a glass of their Grand Patron (a rich wine from old Carignan vines) to accompany the braised lamb from the tajine, he began to explain that the Muslim ethos extended to other company practices too. As with all of the visits so far, the business was a joint venture between Tunisians and export partners. Domaine Atlas's European partner had initially put forward suggestions for cost saving and maximising profits – measures at the core of every self-respecting business plan in the West. These involved vineyard mechanisation, as well as getting rid of less profitable activities such as the olive groves and citrus plantations. This didn't sit well with the Tunisians' desire for the high level of employment created by hand-harvesting a variety of produce throughout the year. It seemed that as long as the business made enough profit to ensure its continuation, then the people were its priority. I pondered the reaction from friends in the UK banking industry at the suggestion that their companies do the same. I was going native!

A respect for the Tunisian approach turned to a desire to disassociate myself from anything English towards the end of our meal. Not having been to Gravesend, I can't vouch for what sort of place it is. It may well have some lovely spots the local tourist board is busily trying to promote, though instead of spending money on advertising, they should be withholding the passports of some of its residents – the four that then pulled up at the winery would be a start. When I worked in hotels, a click of the fingers and a shout of 'oi garçon' would have led to my being sacked – assaulting a guest not being permitted. Imed's response was immaculate. Although it was not a restaurant he asked them to sit for lunch, as his guests. He was mercurial throughout, responding to requests made of him without question, only failing in being able to provide Heinz ketchup. He offered them a tasting, which they accepted with gusto – the designated driver indistinguishable, having presumably cottoned on that there were no drink-drive laws.

As Imed sat back with us for a moment, I applauded him and admired the Muslim approach. He winked and said it was marketing, Muslim-style. He then placed an order pad on their table as they tasted, which was quickly put to work. Even the winery staff, as they wheelbarrowed the cases to the back of the van, displayed an air of disbelief at the volume leaving the storeroom. This, we were told, would be taken back to a resort in Hammamet: not the fruits of Dover's most ambitious booze-cruise.

We were about to broach the now routine question as to where might be a suitable place to camp that night, when Imed pre-empted the request. 'I understand you are sleeping on your roof. Please stay here, you will be quite safe, unless of course you have other plans.' Having none except writing up a few notes, we accepted. Imed explained that as Sunday was the only day he saw his children, he would be going as soon as the groaning van had left. He asked if we would mind if he left us with the keys to the kitchen, saying we should find all we needed there for an evening meal, as well as a selection of bottles from which to choose. If we required anything our guard would be delighted to go into Hammamet for us.

The little courtyard, so animated before, echoed only to the twitter of finches after everyone had left. The mother of a young brood in the rafters seemed to resent my presence as I sat with my laptop, though others were quite content to peck at the ground under Philip as he lay asleep on a bench. The straw canopy absorbed the heat from the afternoon sun and a mountain breeze rustled my papers. A full stomach made writing a slow process and I was soon snoozing at the keyboard.

'Chicken!'

Our guard apparently was not questioning my bravery as he poked my arm a little later; but instead seemed to be saying that he was going into town to get some food and would we like some. I said yes please and would he like me to come. He somewhat firmly insisted that it wasn't necessary. Philip awoke too and suggested that we do a little filming outside, so, when our guard had left, we drove through the hole in the hedge and a little way up the mountain. I'd say a few words to the camera and then we'd return for the food and a glass of wine.

We had the perfect backdrop in the viewfinder. The sun lit the deserted valley a warm gold; prickly pear lined the road's edge and the lush green of the estate's vines could be seen some way down the slope. As I began to speak, a shepherdess with her flock appeared in shot along the road, lending the scene depth. This impression of tranquillity was somewhat shaken as she began to stride towards us, wildly waving her stick when she saw the camera. Had we stolen her soul? We turned off the offending article and walked to meet her, prepared to destroy the tape should we need to. It soon transpired that it was not her spirit she was concerned with, but her membership of Equity – she wanted money to be filmed. She patted her palm and mentioned a figure that I told her would have Meryl Streep blushing. Although she didn't know who the actress was, she was prepared to haggle. In fact, it seemed to be more about the haggling than the money as we went from one figure to another, she with a grin on her face. She settled for a more modest amount and went back into position, though not before unexpectedly pulling out a mobile phone and making a call. She then gave a wave that we thought indicated she was ready for her piece, though I now suspect it was a clandestine signal for others to join the cast. What had been a lonely mountain road turned into scene from a biblical epic, albeit one with a soft drink truck weaving among the hoards marauding into shot. We packed the camera away in fear of the impending wages demand and fled, choosing to film back at the estate without a cast.

The guard returned with the chicken a short while later and

evening slipped into night on the veranda as we ate. The speed at which our guard became drunk as he sipped suggested that wine was unfamiliar territory for him. We hoped that Allah would forgive him under the circumstances.

* * *

Having driven in Rome at rush hour I had thought I would be prepared for Africa, though Latin driving is closer to that in the Cotswolds than to Tunis. I employed the 'only care about the front half of your vehicle' method of driving adopted in London and hoped it might see us through. Most of the traffic lights worked, though what they were controlling was less clear. The police at the roundabouts encouraging drivers to ignore them were the ones to obey.

'Come into Tunis and ask for UCCV,' had been our directions – even after we requested something more detailed to guide us into a city of three million people. We were fortunate enough to ask a driver of a pickup who was actually heading there and only noticed UCCV emblazoned on his tailgate as he pulled ahead. The wide central boulevard, a relic of the colonial era, led to a grid of indus-trialisation on an epic scale: cement works with aviation warning lights, refineries whose tangled pipe work sprawled for blocks on end, and trucks the size of houses that dwarfed our car. A little more respect for other road users was needed here, now we were the smallest. We followed the pickup into a courtyard about as far removed from the one we'd left that morning as it was possible to be. At its centre was a neatly clipped green with scenes of high activity surrounding it. Forklifts whisked between vast trailers in a seemingly choreographed performance. Pipes led to a road tanker either loading or unloading wine, or was it fuel? Above the administration block stood a scaffold bearing the letters UCCV, which, when combined with the clipboards, white coats and uniforms, gave the square a somewhat utilitarian feel. A military dictator might not have appeared out of place on the balcony.

We drew up under the Tunisian flag that adorns all government buildings and were met by Abdelmoula, the company's export manager. He would be leading us on a tour of their various estates. His impeccable English as he greeted us made me realise that I could be lazy and revert to my mother tongue for the next two days. Here was another man who was clearly used to handling visitors, and others more important than us, judging by the deference other staff gave him, the first of whom was our appointed driver for the visit. He was under the bonnet of a dusty staff car. Abdelmoula said a few words to the man, looked about, and then returned to us.

He explained that UCCV (Union Central des Coopératives Viticoles), or Vignerons de Carthage, is the oldest and largest wine producer in Tunisia, accounting for around sixty per cent of the market. The company became state owned after Independence and now has a wide range of its own estates along with overseas partnerships. He was keen to list a selection of countries to which they export and explained, somewhat expectantly, that the list excluded the UK. I think my influence had somehow been misunderstood. He looked across to the car again and invited us to a coffee before we started our tour of the company's properties. We were led up a broad flight of steps and past the reception area into a gleaming office. The patina of polish added a few millimetres to every surface, including the thick leather armchairs that crackled as we sat on them. These seemed to date from the same era as the colonial map on the wall, also made of polished hide. Abdelmoula looked out of the window, observing the square. We sat and waited.

Two shelves in a wall-wide cabinet displayed a range of bottles. The labels on the upper shelf seemed ancient relics in terms of design compared with those in the lower one so I asked whether these were from 1948 when the company started. He eyed me a little intensely as he explained these were the labels used until a re-brand a couple of years ago. I was probably a little excessive in my appreciation of the new ones in response. I turned my attention to an impressive array of awards the wines had received in competitions, though the pride of place was reserved for an 'ISO 9001 version 2000' certificate in a gilt frame, which the company was awarded in 2005 after a re-fit. I hoped that I expressed sufficient awe (as the award has more to do with equipment installation than wine quality). I asked to use the loo, which should itself have had an 'ISO 9001 version 2000' certificate – a magnificent piece of porcelain finer than anything to be found in France. When I returned, Abdelmoula had gone and in his place were the coffees. A glance from the window confirmed that he was in the courtyard assisting the driver, though the latter seemed not to appreciate it as such. The bonnet was lowered and he returned to us, asking whether we would like to begin our tour.

The driver seemed a little anxious as he drove us out of the courtyard and down the road, as if he wasn't convinced of something. As if on cue the car's alarm went off and we drew to a halt in an adjacent yard. This also belonged to the company and a large balding man stepped from a workshop, flipped the bonnet, wiggled a few wires and we were off again – for three blocks. Two hours into our visit we had arrived at our first destination: the rear of a warehouse at the end of an alley. A sagging chain-link fence abutted a piece of wasteland beside us and two scrawny dogs foraged behind some bins. I was beginning to wonder whether it had been wise to organise this visit at all – a couple of days on one of Hammamet's beaches now seemed more appealing.

We were led into the building and between two columns of vast cement tanks to a small door. The door was opened into the darkness beyond and we were encouraged down a flight of dimly lit steps.

The awe one feels at being led through the grotto-like cellars in Burgundy could be a little diminished by a level of expectation. The scenes here at street level had left me with no expectation at all, so the labyrinth tunnelled deep beneath the winery couldn't have impressed more. Anyone who has been in a cave will know the dank smell of moist rock, and some will like it and some will not; but when that smell combines with the aromas of maturing wine and the sweet vanilla scent of new barrels, I've yet to find someone who isn't seduced. We walked some way along a tunnel lined with bottles full of maturing wine before it opened into a cavern lit with candles. Barrels occupied every inch of floor space, except for where a table with a full decanter and glasses stood.

Whilst the caves only date from colonial times, the name of the wine in the barrels and decanter harks back to a much earlier era in Tunisia's history. They contained the pinnacle of the company's production, Vieux Magon. Magon was the finest winemaker of his time. A resident of Carthage in the eighth century BC, he pioneered some of the vineyard and winemaking processes that the Romans would later use as they spread the vine throughout Europe. (As well as pinching his ideas when they arrived, they made a bit of a mess of Carthage too.)

I closed my eyes as I began to taste, something our hosts might have taken as an effort to focus on the wine. I was in fact visualising the scenes of heavy industry above in order to try and judge the wine objectively. It may have worked; I wasn't sure, as my first note was 'Yum.' The wine was a voluptuous blend of Carignan from fifty-year-old vines and Syrah from those only a little younger, and it had quality that one might only expect when using the very best grapes of a company that has ten thousand hectares of vines to choose from. Packed with powerful aromas of black plum, coffee and cardamom spice, it was a velvet fruit bomb. I even gave it one smiley face to accompany my score. I have occasionally been frowned upon when tasting at a formal occasion for appearing less than suitably sombre, though that's only when I come across a wine that makes me smile and I drink a little of it as well as spit. This is when a wine is not only high quality, but enjoyable – meaning that it's ready to drink and giving its best. Wines unready to drink can still attract a good score, but to attain a smiley face I have to enjoy it too. The maximum three smiley faces are only awarded when, having stolen the tasting sample, I run from the room, shouting 'Woo-hoo!'

This wine was the 2002 Vieux Magon and had only just been released. Abdelmoula said that he'd recently had a 1976 and a 1985 and both still had time to go. I wondered whether they were woo-hoo wines.

After an unconvincing start, the car performed admirably all day, taking us on a series of vineyard visits in Cap Bon that were punctuated by stop at a restaurant in the coastal town of Kirkina. Where I have my woo-hoo with wine, if something appeals to Philip in a gastronomic sense it 'revs his motor'. The little seafood restaurant was in danger of having him blowing a gasket; such was the quality of the octopus and squid starter. So fresh was the former that it almost had to be prised from the salver and the macadamia nut texture of the squid was unlike anything I'd encountered. To apply any celebrity chef-style cookery to any of this simple food would have ruined it. The impact that quality of ingredient has on flavour could be no more highlighted than by the melon at the end of the meal. The flavour was so vivid it was almost a caricature of what I expected it to taste like. The fruit had come from a garden belonging to the restaurant, so it would be unfair to go into a rant about supermarket produce in the UK, but it did highlight the fact that flavour is hard to manufacture, and this applies to grapes too. A piece of soil only has so much it can offer any fruit grown on it in terms of flavour. If the soil is heavily watered and fertilised it can produce a larger quantity (making more revenue from the land), but the flavour has to spread itself further, rendering the resulting product more dilute. This is why a lot of major volume wine brands are a bit boring – but they are not bad wines, just as watery supermarket melons are not bad melons. They are simply less interesting ones.

The end of our first day complete, Abdelmoula drove us to the accommodation the company had kindly provided. I hadn't mentioned the tent when they'd offered to put us up for the night as we were now beginning to show the effects of life under canvas, and I've never felt that dreadlocks really work on a white man. We were to be transported from the ridiculous to the sublime: there'd be no strip washing under a cold tap at the Sheraton, it would be fine food, jacuzzis and chambermaids. Not, I hasten to add, at the same time.

Although we were looking forward to a little luxury, as we arrived in our room I felt that our trip had momentarily ended and we'd left Tunisia. I have often wondered if an individual were teleported into a hotel room belonging to a chain, how long it might take them to work out which country they were in if the soap was removed. These cynical thoughts were banished the moment we saw the list of services available however. Having saved on hotel bills so far, we would avail ourselves of pretty much everything but the babysitting service. As we prepared to use the gym, our burgeoning bag of dirty laundry was whisked away to be ready for the following morning, pressed and folded. After the gym, we would swim and sauna before dining, making use of the quality end of the wine list. Cost was to be no obstacle!

Cost, however, should have been an obstacle, though it was probably the frivolous attitude brought on by the thought of a hot bath that caused me to overlook the pricing sheet for laundry items. At the equivalent of five pounds for a pair of socks, this was probably a service reserved for Bill Gates. The oversight was only brought to my attention the following morning, after the three chambermaids had finished staggering under their burdens and deposited the laundry on our beds. Looking at the bill, I considered that it might be cheaper to leave the laundry and buy everything new.

'The bill has been taken care of sir.'

I tried to explain to the receptionist that the room was being paid for and that sundries were our responsibility, but she was adamant that it was normal for the bill to be charged to the company account, and it had been done. When Abdelmoula arrived I mentioned the laundry, to which he replied it was on the company. Maybe I didn't sufficiently impress upon him the volume involved, as his expression changed somewhat as he signed the bill off. He quickly regained his composure, though still seemed a little distracted as we drove off. Philip sought to ease the situation with a little conversation.

'Is there a drugs problem in Tunisia?'

'Sorry?'

'Do you have a lot of drugs in Tunisia?'

'No, drugs are highly illegal and there are severe penalties,' he replied.

'And is there an issue with pornography?'

He seemed equally surprised by the question and explained that there were similarly severe penalties for pornography. It was the shock at Phillip's question regarding prostitution that made us realise our host seemed to think that we were trying to add to the hotel bill.

His mood lightened with reassurance, but still I decided to stick to less contentious issues and asked him whether he'd celebrated Tunisia's victory in the African Cup of Nations the week before. He seemed a little confused, saying that the tournament didn't start for another two weeks. We insisted that they had beaten Morocco 2-1 in the final, something widely celebrated on the ferry. He explained that the match had taken place in 2004 and whilst he had indeed enjoyed it, he was more of a rugby man. I now felt a little foolish for offering my hearty congratulations to the barman on board, though he readily accepted them in the manner of someone else who didn't realise he was watching a replay – maybe he wasn't much of a football fan either. After a few minutes banter about the last rugby world cup final between England and South Africa, Abdelmoula mentioned that he had played for the Tunisian national rugby team himself: another modest man.

We were heading out of Tunis to the vineyards one last time, the ancient fishing village of Kélibia on the north-eastern coast of Cap Bon our destination. The town has one of Tunisia's few Premier Cru appellations for its Muscat and we had heard good things about the Chardonnay too.

There barely seemed a patch of land not growing some form of fruit or vegetable as we drove up the spine of the peninsula; a colourful roadside display of avocado, citrus and buckets of red prickly pear marking our progress. I asked whether the area also produced tropical fruit and reeled off a list to Abdelmoula, to which the answer to all was 'naturally'. I tried to name a fruit that wasn't grown, but without success. It seemed I would have to make one up to get one over him, but having just got back into his good books, I thought better of it.

A petrol stop allowed time for an ahwa arabi, the thick gravelly coffee that should be prescribed as a cure for narcolepsy. The simple booth was unencumbered with any decoration save for the ubiquitous poster of the president. As Abdelmoula handed out the coffees and drew up a plastic chair, I asked him whether the posters were provided by the state or had to be bought. It seemed that every public amenity, be it restaurant, corner shop or petrol station, had the choice of three different shots of Zine El Abidine Ben Ali. Having never won less than 94 per cent of the vote in the four elections since 1987, he is clearly a popular man, though choice could be described as restricted. Although he is much admired for creating economic success and stability, some say that there is still a little work to be done in areas of freedom of speech (Reporters Sans Frontières – not me, naturally!).

'They were bought out of admiration for him, of course! Now, are we here to discuss wine, or the president?' Along with drugs, pornography and prostitution, I added politics to the list of what not to discuss. I prudently threw in religion for good measure.

We arrived at the company's office in Kélibia and Abdelmoula explained that there was something we should see here before moving on to a winery. Karim, the office manager, was a bit of a disappointment: a fresh-faced man in shirt and tie strode to meet us; and not a Jedi Knight. The opening scenes of Star Wars had been filmed in Tunisia, and it was apparent that George Lucas had not needed to use much imagination when planning sets. The office buildings and those in the villages we'd passed, with their rounded edges and pale blue doors, might have been the inspiration for Luke Skywalker's home planet.

A strong breeze whipped a cord against the flagpole above us. I asked Karim whether this was the Sirocco, the hot wind that comes off the Sahara. At other estates we'd visited we'd been told it was a factor reducing quality in some years – the wind overly stressing the vines and so hindering grape development. He pointed out that the wind was in fact coming from the sea and had a cooling influence. He explained that this was why they'd chosen to plant white grapes there (they generally require cooler climates to do best). Whilst we had tasted many perfectly drinkable whites so far, it was the reds that had stood out. Abdelmoula had scheduled a tasting for a little later and I wondered whether these whites would stand up to scrutiny.

Although the French were responsible for much of what we'd seen in terms of grape varieties, Abdelmoula said he had brought us here as he wanted to show us some Tunisian grapes that might impress. We said goodbye to Karim and we were led into a sandy vineyard. Although the sea was out of sight, we could hear waves pounding on the beach beyond a windbreak. We followed a track to a set of crumbling buildings. Saplings grew through the roofs and creepers scaled the stone walls. An old man wearing a worn blue apron and carrying a chisel appeared at a doorway. Rolling a cigarette, he joined us as we made our way through some long grass (one of us stamping all the while) to an area surrounded by a collapsed wall. I wondered how best to fake being impressed when we saw the grapes.

An American friend once said that if some of the everyday buildings he knew in England were transported to the US, they would be surrounded by high security and charge admission. I had a similar thought as we looked through a gap in the wall across a vibrantly coloured mosaic floor. The size of the area covered by the tiny tiles was much greater than the relics I'd seen in Sussex – the owners of which charge the sort of entrance fee that makes you wonder why they couldn't afford to rebuild the temple.

'This is Carthaginian, and over there you can see proof that we were making wine long before the Romans or French came,' said Abdelmoula, pointing to a corner. Not being able to see anything, Philip and I walked over to the spot and started filming. I described what we'd been told to the camera, pointing to an ornate grape and amphora design in the tiles. Archaeology not having been an option at school, I initially chose to accept that they were genuine, though the fact that we were standing on them gave me cause to doubt it. I asked whether, if the floor were over two and a half thousand years old, it should be protected.

'Yes of course it is. No one is allowed on there ...' He continued forebodingly, 'There are severe penalties!'

Our look of shock must have suitably mimicked his own a little earlier, as he burst into laughter. He was joined by the old man who laughed so much that he dropped his cigarette on the tiles and ground it onto what appeared to be a dish of fruit. Once we were back in the car and on our way to the winery, I pondered that visitors to a museum in Tunis might one day look at the subtlety of the amber shade lent to one of the mosaic's apples, not knowing that it was a tobacco stain. The floor had been discovered when digging had begun for the winery and it had yet to be transported to its new home, where more people could appreciate it. In the meantime another site had been chosen for the winery building that we were about to visit; or at least that was the plan.

A protracted, and buttock-clenching, overtaking movement had put a slow-moving convoy piled high with sugar cane behind us and before I'd had time to remove my fingernails from the seat leather we careered off into the winery grounds. I would have congratulated our driver on his spatial awareness in missing the petrol tanker by what felt like millimetres, though I was too dumbstruck to talk. Whilst this may sound like criticism of our driver, it is actually meant as praise for Tunisia's driving tutors. Surely untrained novices couldn't pull off the many feats of automotive daring that we'd witnessed during our trip.

For a new building, the winery had been cunningly disguised as one much older, or maybe the cleaner was taking some time off. A layer of dust gave the windows a coating that might protect them from impact, and sand drifted against the outer walls. As Abdelmoula went to the door, I approached a window and peered through. Thick plastic sheeting protected three enormous presses, and birds flew about between the tanks, the doors of which, being open, indicated we were in for a dry visit. Abdelmoula's fruitless attempt to open the door and shouts through the letterbox suggested that everyone else was probably with the cleaner. I was a little surprised when he and the driver persevered by walking around the building seeking another entry point, as I wasn't entirely sure why he might want us to see the place at all. After a failed attempt at lifting a shutter with a branch, and the driver's refusal to shimmy up the drainpipe, Abdelmoula made a phone call and conveyed his frustration to someone at the other end. As Philip and I sat on the kerb – the surf breaking in the distance almost taunting us – I told myself that at least we'd had a good day yesterday. After all, our hosts didn't have to spend any time with us at all. I considered my freshly ironed boxer shorts, which was enough to inject a little humility.

Abdelmoula rejoined us, explaining that someone was being sent out with the keys. At this point, to say 'it really wasn't necessary' might appear rude, so we instead conveyed relief. Before long an aged taxi deposited a flustered colleague of Abdelmoula's outside the winery. Fumbling with an assortment of keys that would have necessitated a two-day induction programme, he greeted us and apologised to Abdelmoula. We waited expectantly as he selected a key and entered it into the lock. Had he begun to turn it, his arm would no doubt have been pulled from its socket. The door swung inwards, and what appeared to be the twin of the old man at the mosaic strode out. He made to 'high-five' Abdelmoula as he passed, though a lack of response sent the man on his way with a shrug into the waiting taxi. I began to laugh. Philip apparently appreciated better than I that this was not a time for hilarity and kicked my shin to stop me offending our host. Abdelmoula was thankfully still staring at the open door and didn't notice me wiping my eyes as we prepared to go in.

As we followed in his wake across the winery floor, Abdelmoula explained that this facility was used at harvest time only, and all of the wine was aged in Tunis. This added somewhat to my wonderment as to why we were here, but the speed of his progress suggested that our presence was not for a winery tour at all. He asked us to wait in the hall for a moment and disappeared through a door at the far end.

On closer inspection, beneath the plastic covers and dust was a very modern operation that, with a splash of water and a scrub, would be quickly operational when the grapes arrived at harvest. I lifted the cover off an enormous panel of lights and dials and took a photo, just as Abdelmoula returned. He put down a box he was carrying and strode over. I expected that this might be the end of our association, though he beamed and asked if we'd like to be in the photo with it. Much as I admired the piece of equipment, it would be a snap that would cement any onlooker's belief that I had taken wine-geekdom too far, so I politely declined.

The box Abdelmoula had brought in had been dropped off by a colleague and contained the estate's wines. He explained that we would be taken somewhere nicer to open them. Clearly a fan of juxtaposition, he drove us to the coast and a restaurant built on a rocky outcrop beneath the dramatic hilltop fort of Kélibia. The open-air dining area overlooked the sea, and the bleached wooden tables were fixed into the stone itself. He selected a table away from the spray and began to open bottles. It was another stunning location for a tasting but I decided to leave serious note taking until I again had a chance to taste the wines back at home, a decision assisted by the langoustine, calamari and Carpaccio of Mirou that were presented with the wines. The seafood would only confuse the palate. The Chardonnay from the vines we'd seen earlier was crisp and well made, certainly very pleasing in situ, and I was even unable to disagree with Abdelmoula when he conveyed an appreciation of his own Muscat with a look of delight that only one's wife should witness.

On our way back to Tunis I began to consider our trip so far and the fact that our visits had broadened my understanding of what was possible on the margins of the wine world. Australia was considered to be on the margins until the eighties, and back then, apart from a few mavericks creating what would one day become icons, even most Australian winemakers themselves knew they were making average wines. When the majority started to make wine in a new, non-French, way to suit local conditions, things began to change and the world took notice. Those now making the best wine in Tunisia are those thinking in Tunisian rather than French. I wondered what the future had in store for the country and whether Morocco would live up to what we'd found here.

As he dropped us off by our car, Abdelmoula asked whether we would like to spend another night at the Sheraton. We declined, I expect to his relief, as we wanted to spend our last night in Carthage and see the remains of the Phoenician and Roman civilisations. A vague recollection of schoolboy history suggested it might be somewhere not to be missed. The name conjured images of temples and amphitheatres, though it transpired that a memory of a school lesson largely forgotten is not the sole basis on which to conduct a visit. A guidebook helps.

Having thanked Abdelmoula for his generosity we headed the few miles north towards Carthage. We applied our trusted method of asking the locals for directions a number of times, though now without success. Initially a shopkeeper misunderstood my translation of the word ruins and directed us some way out of Carthage to a dilapidated housing estate. We returned and stopped to ask some uniformed guards parading in front of two vast gates. As this turned out to be the rear entrance to the presidential palace our presence elicited a similar response to an Arabic registered vehicle stopping outside 10 Downing Street. After asking others with similar reward, we began to wonder if there was anything of historic Carthage left. The Romans, it seemed, had done a fairly good job of eradicating traces of the original Phoenician civilisation, and the Vandals in turn had left little of what the Romans had replaced it with. (The Vandals were related to the Goths, which is presumably why you can still find the latter smashing up bus stops.) We had decided to give up when we spotted a stall selling 'Carthage Artefacts'. Those were the words written on the banner above the trestle, but I suspected the artefacts were not as authentic as was claimed. The coins cost only five dinars, less than their original face value (not accounting for two thousand years of inflation); the amphorae were suspiciously unmolested by time; and I'm sure that, had Roman swords been inflatable, the empire wouldn't have been nearly so successful in its sacking of Carthage. We pulled up anyway to ask for directions.

Philip had earlier mentioned that he wanted a new pair of shoes, and I now made the error of pointing some out. I'd known that the six-inch pointed toe with golden tassel might not appeal, and that puce was not Philip's favourite colour, though the stallholder took my mock interest as genuine. He forcibly sat my friend down and began to remove his walking boots. Philip began to complain, but his protestations were taken as a desire to try out the entire range. I tried to interject on his behalf, though it would have taken a hostage negotiation team to extract him. I decided to resort to bribery. I offered the man some fruit, to no avail. He pointed to the car. This was hard bartering – a Land Rover in return for not buying some footwear was steeper than I'd expected. Fortunately I was mistaken, as he just wanted the jacket in the back window instead. It was no deal however. Either Philip would be wearing footwear that would embarrass Julian Clary or I would be continuing the tour solo.

Philip rummaged in his backpack and handed his captor a white bag containing a latticed pastry, which secured his release without purchase. We asked the man where the ruins of Carthage were and he pointed to a wall next to the Land Rover. Standing on top of the vehicle gave us a view of something akin to a reclaimed masonry yard in Peckham. If you like your architecture grand, I thought, stick to Luxor or Athens. This, I hasten to add, is not official tourist advice as I believe there is a little more for the more dedicated historian (one with a map) to see, though we would not have time to visit it, nor indeed the site over the wall, as it had closed whilst we were at the stall. Philip pulled out the camera and filmed through the barbed wire anyway, though I felt that the *History Channel* wouldn't be too impressed with our piece on Carthage if we tried to submit it.

We asked if there was a hotel nearby. He pointed in one direction and rubbed his thumb and forefinger together to indicate expense, then pointed in the other and exclaimed, 'Luverly jubbly mate!' Clearly delighted by our surprised reaction to his grasp of English culture, he shook us both warmly by the hand and waved us off. As we drove on, Philip split a second pastry and shared it between us. The cheese and onion slice (bought in France a week earlier) had lost none of its gastronomic impact, though I'd been expecting ham and cheese. The guilty smile on Philip's face suggested that the pork-based filling had indeed been used in the transaction. The sense of guilt at proffering taboo meat was dispelled when we arrived at the hotel, however. It seemed that our friend had had the last laugh.

Finding a parking space outside the hotel was not a problem. There was only one other vehicle: a courtesy bus with a 'police aware' sticker (it may have said something else, but I doubted it). A vast water feature that for some years would have only seen action in a downpour dominated the courtyard, and one of the balconies had tumbled into the swimming pool below. The Sheraton this was not, but it wouldn't cost a great deal more than camping. A receptionist looked up as we pushed open the no longer automatic doors. He welcomed us and pointed out the amenities, which comprised working air conditioning, a lift and a private beach; the latter, little more than a sandpit fenced off by rusting iron railings, had its own shipwreck. He was keen to point out that this didn't belong to the hotel, so was out of bounds. For anyone in particularly good humour the hotel was fascinating, though it wouldn't be the place to go if you felt less than contented with your lot in life.

After having deposited our bags in a bedroom just large enough to accommodate them, we took the lift down to the basement bar. I commented on a strong reek of TCP in the lift compartment and Philip mused that they probably had an issue with cockroaches. As the lift door opened, however, it was clear that the creatures had developed immunity, as two of them were facing the doors waiting to get in. Philip quickly dispatched them and pointed the remnants out to a member of staff. Rather than taking the gesture as a form of complaint, the woman seemed genuinely distressed at their demise and walked away – presumably we had killed the hotel's pets. As we ordered a beer we consoled ourselves that they would likely have others.

Strangely, the bar was full. We assumed that the severe penalties Abdelmoula had spoken of earlier were no deterrent to the women and their clients in the bar. Incensed smoke hung in the air, perhaps deployed as some form of screen to hinder detection, so we left for the restaurant. Once away from the bar the air cleared again to reveal the smell of a long-deserted hospital ward. A sign for the restaurant led us through a vast ballroom, complete with a many-tiered chandelier that seemed not to have twinkled for years. Dusty tables and chairs were stacked to one side. The echoes of our feet were joined by the noise of a raised voice beyond an archway into another room. Although the words were indiscernible, the language had the rolling twang of southern France rather than the more clipped French spoken by Tunisians. It also had the gravel of a voice ground down by cigarettes, alcohol and hard living. A waiter appeared through the archway and hurried passed us, as if dispatched on an errand.

Entering the room gave me cause to throw off my cynicisms and believe in fate. There in the dimness of the furthest corner, alone and hunched over a table overlooking the sea, was the characteristic shape of a man I had last seen in a London television studio. His features in the half-light were unmistakeable: the straw blond hair, prominent jawline and distinguishing nose gave me no cause for doubt. This was the man I was looking for! I walked towards him and took a seat at his table. He looked confused. I began to remind him of our having met, but he failed to recognise me. I conceded to myself that the contents of the empty bottle in front of him had taken their toll on his memory. I persevered even as he got up to leave. I was convinced that his protestations were a desire to protect privacy and continued to badger him until Philip led me away, pointing out that he looked nothing like Gérard Depardieu.

He was a Gauloises salesman from Toulon, drowning his sorrows after a less than successful trip. Such is a mirage to a man seeking water, or, in my case, wine.

We left him in peace and ordered our meal and a bottle of Magon Majus. The wine was still delicious, though didn't quite compensate for the quality of the food. Philip gave the restaurant a Michelin tyre rating, an accolade South Africans reserve for chefs that displease them.

Out of Africa – France and Spain

Standing in front of an empty customs kiosk (feeling a little foolish, as the manned kiosk, complete with queue, was the next one along), I watched a lady in tears explain that she'd neglected to put her dog into quarantine before the ferry crossing to France. The official removed his spectacles, rubbed his eyes and gravely asked how large her dog was. She held her hands four feet apart. He smiled broadly, stamped her ticket and called 'next'. This seemed delightfully hassle-free compared with the pet-passport system in the UK, though I wondered whether a dog would need to be smaller or larger to be rejected. At that moment the shutters rolled up in front of me and I was asked for my passport – much to the astonishment of the people in the queue next to me. While I was standing at the back of the queue a few moments earlier a scruffy man had asked me for some change and, when I had given it, he had dragged me to the point in front of the empty kiosk. He had known it was about to open. I still had not got used to the 'fixer' culture at checkpoints. It seemed that the regular officials tolerated them as it meant fewer questions and an easier life for them, even if the fixers were often enterprising in the way they earned their cash.

The return crossing back to France, from where we'd be driving into Spain, and the ferry for Morocco, was virtually deserted; presumably there being no football screening scheduled. The cool sea air had cleansed the boat, leaving no trace of the hookah smoke from before. It seemed that this time we could settle down without fear of being moved on. This was the case for some hours, as I typed up notes and Philip reviewed the Tunisian tapes, but a shadow was cast upon us as the bar opened for business. This was not the pall of smouldering tobacco but that of a Berber lute player who had been instructed to perform to the ship's guests, whether they liked it or not. The barmen seemed to be entertained by the music, which, to my untutored ear, was a masterful impression of a man castrating a cat with piano wire. It seems that an Englishman's look of abject horror can be easily mistaken for one of appreciation, and the player maintained the confident air of an entertainer wooing the devoted.

Packing our things and leaving for the other end of the ship did not sway the man from his purpose. Whilst not quite prancing as the lute player in *Monty Python and the Holy Grail*, he followed in our wake until we finally found somewhere he presumably considered an unsuitable performance arena. After spending ten minutes in the loo we checked to see if the corridor was clear. He had gone and we were safe. Opposite was one of the restaurants, which, being dark, might provide a safe haven. We entered. After some moments the lights behind a service counter flickered on and a waiter approached with menus – maybe ferry restaurants have sensors and only function if you enter, a little like an automatic loo flush. Foolishly, we ordered. The food turned out to be good, but it meant we were now immobile, trapped. Our worst fears were realised seconds later as the sound of tortured strings intensified in the corridor. Eerily, it stopped just outside the frosted doors. Our tormentor's outline could be seen, presumably checking some form of radar he'd been equipped with. The doors burst open and he came at us like a reunited lover. We considered leaving our mussels and wine and returning to our previous sanctuary, but the Kélibia Chardonnay was too good to pass up for a night in a urinal – faint praise perhaps, though without the wine there would have been no contest. He sat at the other end of the room on a low stage, which made the din slightly more tolerable. A few moments later the waiter asked the musician if he would like a drink. He gladly stopped and chatted for some minutes. This gave us an idea. Each time he struck up we asked the waiter a question to convey to the musician, which had the desired effect of pausing the performance. Having asked where he played, who his favourite lute players were, and what he thought of the sad under-exposure of such a noble instrument, he seemed thrilled at the attention. He presumably now thought we were lute A&R men scouting for talent and played with even more effort. Having run out of questions, I tried a request. His two thumbs up and toothy grin announced that he'd heard of Led Zeppelin and would give 'Whole Lotta Love' a go! Now this was worth the price of the ferry ticket alone I thought, but, just as he stood up and adjusted himself to a more fitting pose, the ship's captain and crew walked in and took their place at the centre table. The lute player, realising that he may never again be commissioned for the ferry gig, sat and resumed torturing his Berber repertoire. I considered shouting 'Iceberg!' to put the sailors back to their stations, though simply sat wondering who on earth sailed the boat in their absence.

* * *

An impatient car horn honked somewhere behind us. I considered 'flipping the bird' or whatever one does in these situations to convey irritation (no, I don't know where the phrase comes from either, or indeed 'smacking the pony' or 'bludgeoning the aardvark'), but instead waited for Philip to climb onto the bonnet in order to retrieve the péage ticket. The kit on the roof was high enough to trigger the sensor telling the machine that a truck had pulled in, causing the ticket to be dispensed somewhere in the ether above us.

We had planned an overnight stop rather than complete the 1,100 miles from Marseilles to Algeciras in one go, and the location had been chosen with a familiar theme. Banyuls is a French wine town little known by tourists and long may it remain so. I sometimes don't understand a travel writer's desire to popularise a charming town. It only adds to tourism (and higher prices if it makes a wine). So, having said that, it was with little anticipation that we would be entering this grim complex of fifties high-rises, with a reputation for producing wine fit only for the violent drunks who frequent the hellish bars.

On the understanding that you're probably one of only four people who will end up reading this book, I'm happy to reveal that Banyuls and its sister Collioure are actually unspoilt coastal nooks. They cling to the hillsides where the French Pyrenees meet the sea and are the last towns on the coast before Spain. Because the autoroute bypasses them on its climb to the border, they remain largely the preserve of locals. The gnarled old Grenache vines clinging to the ledges and slopes behind the towns produce wine every bit as dramatic as the scenery. Grenache is a grape that I knew was being grown in Morocco, and this would be another great opportunity to taste a benchmark.

After having spent five hours on the motorway, we took the exit and wound our way down to the coast. The exposed rock of the vineyard slopes held the day's sun, and wild thyme and lavender drifted on the warm breeze. We rounded a corner and caught our first glimpse of the ancient harbour of Collioure.

For the first time in our schedule the timings had not been organised on a 'just in time' basis and we had an afternoon to enjoy the area. Having not forgotten our French guidebook, we had: checked there was no public holiday; pre-arranged a spot to camp at a nearby cove; arranged a short tour of one of the more prominent wine producers; and booked into a seafood restaurant overlooking the harbour. This was the second restaurant we'd tried: the first was advertising a 'Lute Concert – One Night Only!' – Shame, as the menu had looked good.

Our wine tour was at Domaine du Mas Blanc, considered to be one of the finest producers of Banyuls and Collioure wine. These two regions overlap almost perfectly, though the town of Banyuls lends its name to the port-like red produced in the area, and the dry wines are labelled Collioure. The estate makes both, though it was the Banyuls wines we were particularly interested in, as those are based on Grenache.

Reputation has not gone to the head of Jean Michel Parcé, the second-generation owner of the estate. The cellar, behind a set of modest doors in a leafy Banyuls avenue, is a straightforward working affair, uncluttered by marketing frippery. The tasting left me sure that I could judge just how good any Moroccan Grenache would be. The stars of the impressive range were his examples of Banyuls Grand Cru, which come from selected plots of particularly old vines. The grape really shows what it is capable of when given the concentration imparted by old vines and guided into bottle by someone with the skill of this proprietor. My eyes had been closed when I was tasting and I felt like a blind man being led though a kitchen preparing puddings: steeped raisins, dried plums, damson brandy, cinnamon sticks, boiling chocolate, toffee, butterscotch and all manner of mature candied aromas gave me cause to wonder whether it was possible for Africa to compete.

Due to the organisation afforded by our guidebook, the rest of the afternoon and evening went entirely to plan. The restaurant was faultless – a table overlooking the fortified harbour lay waiting with the pre-ordered speciality: a dish of clams, cockles and scallops with lemon butter; at its side a chilled bottle of white Collioure. Then our little bay, quiet save for the croak of a bullfrog and gentle lapping of the waves, provided an idyllic setting in which to settle for the night. As I walked back to the tent from a glistening shower block I threw the guide into a bin – this was no way for someone seeking adventure to behave!

To make use of the time in the car as we drove through Spain, I had set up the laptop at the back of the vehicle to continue typing up my scruffily written notes. So far I had only transferred those up to Champagne to the computer, and I was concerned that before long I'd not be able to read my scrawl (which seemed, conversely, to improve when I was tasting wine – I made a mental note to improve it more often!). As I clattered away or, in truth, pattered (I must try an old typewriter just for the satisfaction of making a more inspiring noise), Philip turned and asked whether all was to sir's satisfaction. I mentioned something about uniform and he suggested another place for my laptop.

Our feet touched Spanish soil only three times on our day-long journey, at the fuel stops that punctuated the blur of orange groves, cork plantations and rocky plains just inland from the coast. Our ferry was to depart that night from Algeciras, a port on the far side of the Bay of Gibraltar. Until we saw a small exit sign that looked as if it had been made using a child's stencil kit, we had begun to wonder whether the Rock of Gibraltar and its inhabitants still existed. For three hundred miles the Spanish had indicated we were travelling towards Algeciras, though for some reason they had been reluctant to go to the same expense for its equally sized neighbour. I think I could guess why, though on the crossing there were some less aware of the territory's sovereignty:

'Look Mom, isn't that the place where the Spanish speak British?'

'No honey, that's a piece of England.'

'But isn't that near Norway?'

'Yes, but it belongs to England.'

'Why don't the Spanish just take it back?'

'Beats me.'

Enter Gimblett: 'Don't tell anyone, but it's a base for Britain to take the rest of the Spain. What do you think the ships are for?'

'Cool!'

I will omit nationality to avoid adding to stereotype.

Into Africa – Morocco

'Give me your passports and papers! Manchester United! David Beckham! Luverly jubbly!' The last three utterances were intended to be endearing enough to have us handing over our documents without concern. The faintly odorous arm of the shifty looking fixer remained thrust through my open window, though the passports were staying with me. The man rummaged beneath his once-white gown and flashed a poorly laminated card complete with a photo of Omar Sharif, or at least someone who couldn't have less resembled the shrivelled character before us.

An official, possibly used to such reluctance, walked in our direction and nodded to say that we were fine to do as the man recommended. Not happy to be parted from the passports, I followed distrustfully as he went from office to office completing the paperwork on our behalf. The process nearly complete, I began to feel a little guilty, as to have attempted it by myself would have been a source of some frustration.

We had arrived in Ceuta, a Spanish Overseas Territory on the north coast of Africa, and had driven through to the Moroccan border controls. When planning the trip there had been no company in the UK prepared to insure the vehicle for Africa. We were told to buy insurance at the borders. This had worked in Tunisia and when asked for our insurance papers now I enquired where the insurance office was. The fixer pointed in the direction of a small booth, but pulled me back as I began to walk toward it. He explained that it was closed. We were in no great hurry – our first appointment wasn't until the following morning. When would it open?

'Possibly in September.'

Since our schedule did not allow for three months in his company, I asked how we could otherwise obtain insurance. As well-meaning as he may have intended to be in answering 'At the border crossing at Tangiers port', I didn't see it as helpful. He nodded when I said this would mean getting the ferry back to Spain and another to Tangiers. We wouldn't arrive back in time for our first visit; one that I knew could not be rescheduled.

The fixer remained unruffled as my state of mind swung a few notches the wrong side of carefree. He said, because we were his friends, he might just have a solution for us. He suggested I stop kicking the tyre and walked over to the border guard. My hopes lifted as the official nodded at what the fixer was suggesting; there was hope! On his return he said that the guard would let us through the border on the basis we drove directly to Tangiers and obtained insurance there. I could have hugged the man, though being aware of Morocco's laws concerning homosexuality, I decided to shake his hand instead. He beat me to it and held his out. I shook it gratefully a number of times but it wasn't withdrawn. Philip pointed out that he was probably asking for money. His fee seemed reasonable so I gladly handed it over. He followed us past the checkpoint, handing the cash to the guard, and gave us a map and directions to Tangiers. When I asked him whether I might have some paperwork to cover the insurance should we be stopped, he gave me the pitying expression of the omniscient looking upon the naive and suggested that this was something we should strenuously avoid. As we began towards Tangiers Philip pointed out that my pace would more likely single us out, and suggested we could probably get away with driving at more than twenty miles an hour.

The coastal countryside picked up where Spain had left off in terms of terrain, though the Moroccans either have laws prohibiting the type of wholesale property development we'd seen near Algeciras, or they simply had more respect for a scenery stunning in its simplicity. On the short trip over, the light had changed. The sky, now cobalt blue, lent the banded rock formations a luminescence that enhanced their changing colours: ochre turned to maroon, maroon gave way to brown, and then brown to cream as we drove the fifty miles through the mountains between Ceuta and Tangiers. The road was deserted. This steadied my nerve regarding the insurance situation, so much so that we decided to stop and film what could be described as a vortex of eagles. As we were about to round a mountain bend, forty or fifty of them had appeared above us riding a thermal. When one reached the top of the swirling spiral it would swoop down to the bottom and climb again – proof that birds do have fun. Philip suggested he film me driving the car beneath the eagles before disappearing around the corner. He picked out a spot a little way up a slope and set the camera in place. I was to disappear for longer than Philip would have hoped.

I had known that the police presence in Morocco would be similar to what we'd encountered in Tunisia, though I think it fair not to have expected a checkpoint on a deserted mountain pass. The moment I spotted the four armed officers standing by their cars a little way down the valley, I realised I had a dilemma: I risked arousing suspicion should I turn around, as they had undoubtedly seen me; but if I passed them it would then look strange coming back through for Philip. I had to leave him behind for now. This could be another friendship-testing situation.

Mustering the confidence of Richard Attenborough when about to board the bus in *The Great Escape* ('Good luck, Herr Bartlett' rang in my ears), I drove casually toward the checkpoint – if the car could have put its hands into its pockets and whistled, it would have. The guards made no movement though I decided to stop, or rather, the steel spikes stretched across the road made the decision for me. I waited whilst one of them finished an anecdote before attending to me, his demeanour changing in an instant from jollity to that of an uncompromising official as he approached. After answering his first question ('why are you here?') to his satisfaction, I answered his second with a thumbs-up. I had cracked the code for safe passage! He had said with a deadpan face, 'Wayne Rooney?' My approval of the man's favourite English footballer had sent me on my way. My allegiance was to change throughout our trip, though I was lucky no one said 'Glen Hoddle'; that might have stretched things.

A while later, having negotiated an alternative route back through the mountains, I found Philip sitting at the foot of the scree nursing a bleeding arm; his perch had given way whilst waiting. I thought to leave it a while before asking whether he'd got any good footage and we re-traced my route back onto the road to Tangiers.

Tangiers was as bustling and hectic as I had feared. All who were driving, cycling or pushing carts were doing so as if they were vastly over-insured and would welcome a claim. We made it to the office however without incident. Now insured, the journey south towards the coast, where we were going to spend a free afternoon, was positively serene.

The city gave way to localised agriculture, once again providing a colourful backdrop to our journey. The fields were smaller than those we'd seen in Tunisia and most contained a shelter of some sort to house those working the land. The rich red tones of the earth, the lush crops, and the animals working the soil provided a rustic scene whose charm might understandably be lost on those toiling in the fields. The air harboured the scents of fruits and vegetables allowed to fully ripen, which mingled with the saline whiff of the sea as we approached Asilah. Having no guide, Asilah had been selected as a point on the map we hoped might offer food for a picnic. It seemed we had chosen well.

Once in the town, the car slowed to a pace that made it quicker to walk, such was the crowd outside the gates of the immaculate fortress medina. A souk, or market, was under way and I imagined there could be no women at home within miles; or men for that matter, though they were sitting in groups smoking rather than shopping. For the first time in Africa our presence wasn't turning heads. The feeling was cosmopolitan, and amongst the market-going hordes was a smattering of western faces.

We parked the car and wandered with the look of those gaining life experience, rather than that of earnest shoppers. Stalls bowed under the weight of muddy legumes, melon and dried peppers. Pyramids of oranges in shapes and sizes that nature intended sat piled high next to an old juice press. Tubs brimmed with olives, and the meat was so fresh you could walk it home on a rope.

We bought some bread and tomatoes, but, as the stallholders seemed to be charging more from unwary pleasure seekers, we waited to see what the locals paid before buying more. Not afraid of a little competition, every fourth stallholder had chosen to sell spices. I spent some time tasting from improbably high piles of powder whose colours resembled the mountain rocks we'd seen. The smell of many I might have once described as curry, though the scents of coriander, cumin, turmeric and fenugreek were all strikingly individual. To the seller's surprise I began to write tasting notes: mixed spice = hints of oak-aged Shiraz with an undercurrent of old vine Grenache.

We added some fruit and a watery sheep's cheese to our hoard and entered the fortress. The narrow cobbled streets were similarly haphazard to the medinas we'd encountered in Tunisia, though these had a delightfully bohemian air, a remnant of its last invaders. Although not as aggressive in their occupation, after the Phoenicians, Portuguese, Arabs and Spanish, came the hippies. Whilst most of these had long returned to California or Paris and become respectable grandparents (the hippies, that is; the rest are long dead), the occasional whiff of 'exotic' tobacco denoted a hangover from a cult that had once flocked to Morocco for its more relaxed attitude to hashish. Leatherwear, pottery and all manner of highly crafted goods hung from the crooked street walls; the products of artisans greeting you from their open doors. One such entrance led to a vast room where two French women were drinking pastis and discussing their own art, which covered every inch of the walls. They clearly had little need of money, as they made no effort to acknowledge visitors in the gallery. They'd also priced their work as if they loathed losing anything they'd created for fear of having to paint something else, thus leaving less time to smoke and drink. Whilst I may not have admired their art, their lifestyle I did.

A gallery next door made more of an effort to sell its paintings. A hooded man who'd been sitting on a three-legged stool heard us speak then shuffled to an ageing ghetto blaster. In an attempt at targeted marketing he selected some English language music for us. Although it put a grin on our faces, I felt with some art lovers his efforts could prove detrimental – Eminem calling the police gentlemen who perform maternal incest maybe not the best thing to stimulate the buying urge. Maybe it was the rap singer's ironic stance on a police state he appreciated, though as he didn't speak English we suspected it may have been lost on him.

It was time for food. We rashly decided to forgo the idyllic beach just beyond the medina for our picnic as there were others using it (we had become spoiled). So we instead returned to the car and headed for a stretch of shoreline some miles south.

As we drove, Philip handed me a slice of the cheese. Along with most of the food that we had tasted in Africa, the creamy white feta oozed flavour and we quickly finished the lot. Moments later, to Philip's surprise, I gripped the steering wheel and screeched to a halt. The cheese had been pulled from a bucket of tap water! Although this fact concerned my companion less than me, I insisted we took precautionary measures. He didn't protest at my proposed antidote and he also downed a glass of wine. I suggested we have another, just in case. I'm still not sure whether this is the most effective way of preventing food poisoning but it seemed natural at the time; after all, throughout history wine has been used as an antiseptic. The Romans famously added it to water to render it drinkable. Roman wine however was considerably weaker than fourteen per cent Collioure and, already feeling its effects, we decided to drive directly to the beach from where we were, rather than risk continuing on the road. We turned down a rutted track and had driven some way when we stopped at a fork. The dust cloud that had billowed behind us caught up, shrouding us in semi-darkness and, although we had seen no one for half an hour, we weren't surprised when four children materialised though the haze (this being the African way). They gave us the traditional 'You're welcome' greeting – the youngest holding out his hand. We offered them some wine branded pencils but they seemed offended. It was probably just that it was a dull gift for ten-year-olds rather than the alcohol-related branding, as we'd seen plenty of Muslim children sporting Jack Daniel's tee shirts and Pernod caps. A little fruit seemed to compensate and we drove on. From then on we handed out sweets in such situations. I contemplated the effect of trying to do the same in the UK: we'd likely be the subject of a few columns in the *Daily Mail* after a lynching by its readers.

Having grown up near the Eastbourne seafront, with its foot-bruising pebbles and oak groynes, I'd never had the chance of adding 'driving along a beach' to my list of life experiences. If you do have the opportunity, I suggest you try it – law permitting, of course. I wasn't sure whether it was indeed lawful as we bowled along the surf's edge but there was nobody there to mind either way. After some time we encountered a train of donkeys taking sand from the shoreline into the dunes (so that's how they make them!), though these were all that marked our progress along the beach. When they receded out of view as dots in the rear view mirror it was difficult to tell how far we'd come; not that this was something that concerned us as we wound down our windows to allow the spray to cool our faces.

After a stop for food, we looked to the map and decided that we should be close to a village a little way inland. We would put the car through its paces by driving across the dunes and join the road from there. This I now know to have been a rash decision on two counts: first, we were a long way further south; and second, my confidence in the car's (and my own) abilities was somewhat over-ambitious. Although when I bought the car I had undergone an afternoon's off-road tuition (I had even bought a 4x4 magazine – covering it with a copy of *Playboy* to save embarrassment at the checkout), my experience had been limited to trundling along dirt tracks in the Scottish Highlands. It transpired that to tackle sand dunes you should have: spades, matting, special tyres, and, judging by the pictures in my 4x4 magazine, a beard and very poor dress sense. I possessed only the last of these.

At first the going was firm, to use the sporting vernacular, and it had been a joy cresting ridges and plunging the vehicle down sandy slopes. My pleasure at being in the desert hadn't lessened by the time we spotted a tarpaulin shelter in the dunes a little while later. A man was standing outside the shelter. We decided to ask him to pinpoint our location. As we neared we could see he was scanning the sea with a pair of binoculars. Casually dressed in a sun-faded tracksuit, he seemed unsurprised that we had stopped for directions – almost cool, as would be a newspaper seller on a London street corner. However, the pistol tucked under his belt put an end to the comparison. The sight of this kept our interaction briefer than planned – we resolved not to find out what he was doing after all. As we pointed to our intended destination on our map a walkie-talkie crackled from a hook in the shelter. His sun-cracked finger jabbed the paper at a place far from where we thought we were and he pointed to the horizon; apparently the direction we needed to head. As we left, he was barking something into his walkie-talkie, which I now suspect to have been 'They're coming your way!'

We had travelled no more than quarter of a mile when the pleasure of driving on sandy terrain began to diminish. The car's speed began to fluctuate, as if I was momentarily releasing the accelerator and re-applying it. We glanced nervously at one another realising that this was the consistency of the ground changing beneath the tyres. Philip suggested we ought to maintain momentum and get to some firmer-looking sand further ahead. What neither of us had seen, as I increased speed, was the ravine in between.

The past few moments had seen my emotions swing from joy to apprehension as they might on a roller coaster ride, and I completed the simile with a scream like that of a schoolgirl at a funfair: I had spotted the ravine when just feet away. I swung the steering wheel into full lock hoping that the pitiful turning circle would be sufficient. The car slewed sideways – the weighty kit on the roof tipping the chassis at a buttock-clenching angle. The outside wheels came within metres of the sheer edge and took the vehicle to safety before burying themselves into a sandbank, their work done.

'Let's let the tyres down.'

My reaction to Philip's suggestion was probably somewhat influenced by my heart rate.

'Why not just f****** stab them and be done with it!'

He patiently explained that doing so to an extent would give them greater purchase on the sand. As we set about releasing pressure from the valves, we noticed two men approaching some way off. Though little more than specks, the silhouette of a rifle on the back of one of the men suggested they were acquaintances of the man we'd met. This hastened our work. Our first attempt to move the car had no more success than gaining six inches back the way we'd come, leaving the rancid smell of smouldering clutch hanging in the air. We dug behind the wheels with our hands and looked for anything we could lay there to aid traction, but there was only more sand. Our next effort won us another two metres. At this rate we would get the car onto firmer terrain by some time the next month. As we began another attempt Philip stopped pushing and looked up. The men were standing next to us. They were younger than the first, probably in their early twenties, and were disturbingly well built.

The man pulled the rifle from his back. Although I could

have improved my pronunciation I felt that this response to my nervous 'marhaban', the Arabic for hello, was a little harsh. He looked at us for some moments then laid the weapon on the ground and joined Philip. His companion poked his head into the cab, checked I had the levers in the right places, then helped the others push. They worked with us in silence, getting us back on firm ground within ten minutes. We wondered how to thank them. Thinking that pencils probably wouldn't be suitable and having gestured towards a bottle of wine without success, we thought to offer some cash. This they declined, pointing to the distance and saying, 'Capitan! Capitan!' There we could see the man we'd first met, still with his binoculars.

Using his walkie-talkie he'd instructed them to guide us, but we had driven into trouble a little too quickly. They were part of an undercover army force that had been stationed there to stop drug smugglers from leaving the coast – thankfully we hadn't fitted the profile! We thanked them warmly and waved to their captain, though as they walked off we couldn't help smiling at the incongruous nature of the 'cigarette' one of them had been smoking.

* * *

I gripped the ledge, fearful that I should be blown into the gorge and dashed onto the rocks a thousand metres below. The wind again gathered pace some way down the valley, so it would soon be enough to pluck my fingers from the ledge and hurl me to my death. I looked down, but what concerned me more than the drop was the fact that I was wearing no clothes and the others climbing the mountain were laughing at me.

I awoke and went for a glass of water.

I didn't need a psychologist to tell me that this was a

symptom of having rashly agreed to take part in the Three Peaks Challenge six days after our return to the UK. My conditioning over the past weeks had put me in shape for some type of gastronomic challenge, though wine and couscous were unsurprisingly absent from the Three Peaks regime. There had been something about taking long walks. We had to leave the lodge where we'd spent the night in a couple of hours, so I had no time for a long walk but could go for another run (in my view the only reason for doing so being not having time to walk). A look in the bathroom mirror confirmed a little exercise could only improve what I saw, so I cleared away the empty glasses from the night before and slipped out of the room via the veranda and onto the beach.

If one ever needed an incentive for a run, it was here. The sun had just crested above the sea and a breeze made the temperature closer to something reminiscent of high summer in England. The beach was a southerly continuation of the one we'd driven on the previous afternoon and it was equally desolate. The texture of the wet sand made the normally arduous process of flinging one leg in front of the other a pleasure and I encountered only a family of cows as I bounded along. I had been gone half an hour when I spotted a man ankle deep in the water a little way ahead, peering at something lurking beneath him. It was time to turn back, but I was too inquisitive to ignore it. He didn't notice me approaching and I gave him a start when I said hello. The effect of the temperature that morning on our attire had been rather different: he walked out of the sea in jeans, a chunky jumper and beaten windcheater, and looked as if to say I must be freezing in my shorts and tee shirt. I pointed to the water and he pulled out some calamari from his pocket and wiped flecks of sand from them. He also took out a coil of fishing line and a bright hook and showed me how he had caught the squid with a series of gestures. He invited me to have a go but we didn't see any. I wondered how long it had taken him to catch them. I could only imagine that he'd been out for most of the night, judging by the state of his clothes. I tried asking him if this had been the case by placing my hands together and putting them by my ear to mimic sleep then pointing to the sand. He seemed unsure what I meant and I motioned not to worry. I thought to give him a little money. We had met others in his situation whose only thought of us was as a potential source of a handout, though he had freely given me his time. Offering the money caused the fisherman to re-think the nature of my question regarding sleeping and he backed away, wildly shaking his head.

It took me some moments to realise that he thought I wanted him to break the law, and a little longer to adequately convey that I would also find it disagreeable. He again approached me with enough confidence to take the money and offered me a smoke of his hashish. My running was erratic enough as it was, and I left him filling his pipe as I returned to the lodge, where there was some good news waiting for me.

Unbeknown to Gérard Depardieu, under Philip's name, we had requested an appointment with an employee of his and had been granted a meeting at the winery later in the week. As we began the journey towards Meknes (the location of our visit later that morning) I considered whether some form of disguise might be appropriate when we visited Gérard's property. Philip, not for the first time, suggested I shave my head. This sparked the usual conversation about hair, and as to whether jealousy has any place in a friendship.

As we neared Meknes, a tickling sensation made me glance at my shorts just in time to see a bee disappear up one leg. Though it should have been, the road was no longer my chief concern as I frantically tried to disrobe at the wheel.

Before the insect had diverted my attention, we had been marvelling at a procession of men spaced along the roadside selling artichokes. We wondered which of them would get the most business. I had thought it would be the first one that people encountered, though Philip thought that by the time you decided you might want some you would have passed the first two. We'd both agreed the tenth would get no trade at all.

Ironically, it was the tenth that we stopped at, albeit somewhat abruptly – the screeching tyres causing the young man to vault the fence behind him in fear of losing a limb. He was unharmed, as were his artichokes. Moreover, I'm pleased to say, so were my prospects of having children again; the bee having flown lazily out of the window, unaware of the near-carnage it had caused (well, I suppose it may have been aware and could have even apologised). Philip however didn't seem as pleased as I was.

'Remember, never let an animal get between you and the road – always keep on course.' He had previously mentioned a statistic that more people are killed whilst trying to avoid stray dogs in South Africa than in any other form of road accident. I explained that had the bee been about to hit the bumper rather than venture into my underpants I would have remained coolly dispassionate. He seemed unimpressed by my logic and said something about it being a butterfly anyhow. As I vowed to let a stray dog loose about Philip's shorts the next time he was driving, the artichoke seller returned and asked if we wanted to buy. The price of an artichoke seemed improbably high but we wanted to compensate for the stress we'd caused, so handed over the amount chalked on the side of the crate. He gave us the crate and walked home. It seemed that the tenth was getting the most business that day.

* * *

We greeted the guard at what we hoped was the entrance to Castel's Moroccan venture. We had bypassed Meknes and driven into a wide valley just off the motorway between Meknes and Fes. We had no instructions other than to look out for vines after our exit, and the vast swathe of neat green rows stretching to either horizon was sufficient to tell us we had arrived, but we couldn't see any buildings. We were told this was the back entrance but we could go in via the vineyard. After ten minutes driving we turned down an avenue shaded by ancient palms. Here, brightly coloured rose bushes ended each row of vines (these being the only ones that visitors using the front entrance would see). Once a feature that would help warn of imminent fungal attack, roses have since been superseded by more scientific methods, though many vine-growers keep them to add a little colour as meteorological forecasts nailed to posts are less attractive. Not that any more colour was needed at the Castel operation. The converted colonial ranch, complete with ornamental gardens, was the unexpected setting for a property that I had thought would be purely functional. There were newer buildings to the rear, but these had skilfully been added without detracting from the ambience.

Although large in Moroccan terms, the Bordeaux firm's operation in the country is just a part of a wide-ranging portfolio employing 3,300 people worldwide. They were one of the first foreign companies to take advantage of the incentives put in place by King Hassan II in 1990 to encourage foreign investment in the Moroccan wine industry. In some markets Castel has changed the perception of Moroccan wine with international styles and modern packaging. I was keen to learn more.

I have occasionally felt that my presence at a winery has

been regarded as unusual and it hasn't concerned me. In fact, it's quite nice not to be one of a procession of individuals asking the same questions. However, the feeling of being out of place here was a little more pronounced.

We were led into a director's office after having waited for some time to be summoned. A stocky man in his fifties pushed back some paperwork as we entered and replaced it with an overflowing ashtray. He tapped a Marlboro from his packet and lit the cigarette. Tilting his chair backward he beckoned us over. We weren't sure whether he wished us to be seated, though we pulled up a couple of chairs and thanked him for sparing the time to see us. He nodded though said nothing and looked from me to Philip and back. He had the air of a kingpin about to be questioned. To get the ball rolling I asked him when the venture was formed. He answered with a level of brevity I was not expecting. I jotted down '1993' and muttered 'very interesting'. Silence reigned. I decided the question had not been open-ended enough.

'How many grape varieties do you have?'

Schoolboy error. I added '8' to my notepad and thought of another question.

'Which ones do you have?' earned me, predictably, another eight words. I felt that asking him where they were planted might occupy him for longer, though I was wrong. He slid over a brochure with a map, seemingly pleased that he could save us both time. He sat silently as I scanned the information searching for an omission that might open up discussion. When I somewhat feebly asked him what he thought of the range, he realised that he had withstood my incisive questioning, and delivered the closing blow. 'I believe people think our wines are nice,' he said, before standing up. I wrote down 'nice' and began to pack my pad away. His countenance brightened at this sign of resignation and he asked if I still wished to see the winery. An affirmative answer sent him through the door for a moment before re-entering with a fresh-faced and somewhat-timid looking man in khaki suit sporting a handsome moustache. The director muttered a few words to his junior colleague, I suspected tips on how to avoid awkward questions, and popped a cyanide pill into his hand (it may have been my card, I couldn't quite see).

Our guide whisked us through a very professional looking operation furnished with a lot of equipment that would make many of the latest New World wineries look dated, fielding questions where he could from the brochure. When I asked one he couldn't look up, he explained he was the office procurement manager and didn't drink wine. It became clear that there wasn't going to be a tasting here. As he led us back across the yard to our car he changed the conversation from the tricky subject of wine to those of religion and George Bush. He seemed perplexed at my lack of the former but was delighted with our attitude toward the latter. It seemed that, as many westerners consider a Muslim stereotype to be the norm, he had thought the religious and political views of the incumbent US President would be those of the West generally. Sadly, it seems those with power often project the stereotype and mortals on both sides are generally closer in ideology than one thinks.

We chatted for a while, as he showed us some photos of his Saharan hometown, then we said goodbye. As we stood by the car I felt a little disappointed that I had not gained more from my visit, though realised I had perhaps been spoilt by the wine industry, where there's more of a tradition of having the curious scrutinise a producer's methods.

* * *

Philip abruptly curtailed his verbal abuse of the mobile broadband toggle he had bought for the trip (something that you stick into a laptop to access the internet from anywhere in the world – supposedly). The little device, sold as a part of the package with his phone, had, according to his service provider, been 're-activated' and 'should be working perfectly'. I was witnessing evidence to the contrary. The veins bulged at his temples as he waved it about contemplating how best to vent his anger, whilst now being patiently watched by a Berber woman who'd materialised out of nowhere (she'd presumably been drawn by the exotic language). Her mode of dress, a shimmering orange jallaba (the traditional Berber smock) seemed at odds with the goats beside her and the brushwood in her hand. Her plain, round, face showed age that was probably ahead of her years. She stood motionless, observing us with a fixed smile as we re-packed the laptop and resigned ourselves to another week without internet access – the sort of hardship that no explorer should have to endure. At the time I imagined she saw irony in the fact that we had so easily come to rely on a technology that would not have been available to us only a year before. But I now know that this was far from what she had in mind.

We had left Castel with a little more time on our hands than anticipated and decided to do some sightseeing. Bereft of a guidebook, we had looked to a map for guidance. A little way to the north of Meknes was the name Volubilis, with an illustration of an eye next to it. There were only a few of these eyes on the map, which we took to mean the location of a place of particular interest. If it did not, we would soon be visiting an optician in the desert.

Having bought the currency of the streets, a large bag of bonbons, Philip offered the woman some. She seemed delighted and pocketed them. Then she placed her hand to her mouth in a sipping motion. She looked crestfallen as I indicated a wish to move on but Philip asked if there was any reason we shouldn't join her for tea. The anticipation on her face, coupled with my companion's intonation that I was being rude, soon had me acquiescing. We had read that it was part of Islamic custom to invite strangers for tea, and I supposed I had initially reacted with the caution of an Englishman. What had we to lose? After we'd entered her house I began to feel there might be a great deal.

She led us a little way up a track to an unremarkable looking house surrounded by a fence of cut thorn-wood. The building was undistinguished for the fact that it was a two-storey square with a flat roof, the house of choice in Morocco. She dragged aside a branch and beckoned us in. The contrast between the outside and inside could not have been greater. The floor and walls were decorated with glazed earthenware tiling, and vivid colour radiated from everywhere, from the hand-dyed curtains to the throws draped across the seating. The colours somehow harmonised, giving the house an inner vibrancy. This was the home of an immensely proud person, and, it turned out, her highly feverish sister. The relative was introduced from a distance. Having no language in common, the woman we'd met indicated that we shouldn't get too close and encouraged us to sit on the opposite side of the room. Seeing the shivering figure, her neck swaddled in sweat-drenched bandages, gave me the desire to be no closer than the opposite side of the valley. Philip seemed to think I was being paranoid. I said that I was not keen to make use of our medical insurance and sat closest to the door, gulping lungfuls of air from the breeze coming in. As the woman, who had introduced herself as Fatima, began to make the tea, I contemplated how best to foreshorten the visit. I thought I had my chance moments later as she disappeared into the garden to gather mint, though I remained frozen by the fixed gaze of the perspiring patient. On her return Fatima may have noticed my state of mind – the ashen face and startled eyebrows possibly giving me away. She tried to explain something in Arabic to us. Our apologetic looks sent her back out of the door. We waited, Philip's calm in contrast to my fleeting looks between the sister and the door.

Moments later Fatima returned with a short man of about thirty-five wearing jeans and a polo shirt. He beamed as he entered, delighted that we had accepted her invitation. In fluent, almost Parisian, French he introduced himself as Rachid, a neighbour of Fatima's. What Fatima was trying to ask, he explained, was, would Philip like to pour the tea? This he did, though apparently not well enough. I could see nothing wrong with the way the green liquid had entered the silver cups from the elegantly spouted pot, though Rachid said it needed to be done from higher up. The tea was tipped back into the pot, and, having elevated his hand, Philip duly poured once again. This too was not satisfactory. Fatima giggled as Philip stood and repeated the process, again without success. A grin on his face, Rachid suggested Philip stand on a chair to perform the action. Fatima clapped as the stream plunged into the cup and frothed over the edges – apparently the way it should be served. Flat tea to a Moroccan is as flat beer to a German. I handed the cups around and, although I thought I showed no sign of hesitation when I reached the sister, Rachid explained that she had just had an operation on her neck tendons and couldn't speak; something I too found difficult as I sipped the tea, its sweetness beyond anything I'd encountered. Noticing me wince, Fatima offered the sugar bowl. I declined and gulped the cup's thankfully limited contents. I was promptly poured another.

Touareg tea, I later learned, has a ceremonial role in Arab culture as well as one of general refreshment. Made with one part fresh mint to five parts sugar added to green tea, it is used to welcome visitors. Pouring is generally the responsibility of the man of the house. This was why, I now realise, the task had been given to Philip. Fatima sat to one side as we drank, on her face the same contented smile as when we'd first seen her. As she stared at my friend I considered whether it was the expletives or the abuse of a communications device that she'd first found attractive in him. Philip seemed oblivious to his admirer as he chatted to Rachid, who I could see was well aware of our hostess's feelings. She leant across and said something to him, prompting an embarrassed cough and relayed question. Did Philip have anyone to clean the house for him in England? Philip thought it an odd question and explained that someone came from an agency once a week. The penny dropped when he was asked if he required more permanent and broad-ranging services. Fatima smiled expectantly. Philip did not. I couldn't help muttering something about not wishing to cause offence. Philip didn't find this helpful and began to think how to best to explain, but Rachid intervened on his behalf, pointing to my companion's wedding ring. Fatima's smile faded and she left the room on the pretext of cleaning the teapot. To save her further humiliation, Rachid told her that Philip and I had an appointment and we said our goodbyes. Outside Rachid said that it was a dream of hers to live in France or England because, she had often said, people led happier lives there. Rachid asked if he might have a lift back to his house, which was a little way up the hill. Little did we know then that this was another ploy!

Beneath a large walnut tree sat three good friends idly joking with one another. Between them was a pyramid of crates about four feet tall and full of citrus, figs, plums and peaches. Every so often one or other would stop talking about football, cars or whatever it was they'd been discussing, and wander to the open window of someone who had pulled up to sell them a quantity of fruit. They seemed to know most of those that stopped by and spent more time in relaxed conversation than in the act of trading. These three were Rachid's father and uncles: the sales force of his business empire.

After we'd sampled most of their produce (having finished a plum or peach, another fruit would be tossed to us) Rachid led us into the garden he had been tending when Fatima had called upon him. There was no corner left uncultivated, and little it didn't support. In addition to the fruit trees that were providing the goods of commerce at the end of the leafy drive, were rows of dark green leeks, cabbages, onions and herbs, next to bushes I didn't recognise – apparently spices. I asked whether there was anything he shopped for. He grinned and said sweets, causing the re-emergence of the packet. We asked about meat and were led to a small cluster of sheds housing everything but, somewhat predictably, pigs. Although he patted a goat fondly as he spoke, a hatchet leaning against a chicken pen left us in no doubt as to the yard's functionality; a fact underlined by Rachid's mother as she leant into the pen, departing with one of the birds and the tool.

The house was full of the smell of baking bread and grilled meat when we entered (mid afternoon being an odd time of day for a meal, we thought) and the sound of elder female relatives could be heard in the kitchen. His father had built the house in the fifties and the areas of greatest importance to the family had been given priority. The kitchen would shame that of a small palace, and the two dining areas, one on the roof and another on a ground-floor terrace overlooking the valley, had been built to afford the best views. We were led through each room, and while it

103

struck me as unusual to be guided around the house of a man we didn't know, we weren't uncomfortable. Rachid proudly introduced his brothers and sisters pictured in frames on a sill, nine in all. There were college graduation photographs, a woman in a suit, two of men in uniform, and one with a young couple outside a large house by the sea. 'That is Mahmoud, he is a barrister in Casablanca, though he is no longer together with his wife.' They had all moved away, leaving Rachid the only sibling at home.

He took us back down to the veranda and invited us to sit at a table that had been set whilst we were in the house. The valley was a patchwork of warm earth tones and the resinous smell of the vine leaves, shading us from the afternoon sun, hung in the air. Rachid's grandmother appeared via a curtained door and laid down a dish of green beans with white onion and herbs, and another piled high with couscous and courgette. The chicken appeared shortly after in a more appealing form than when we had last seen it: simply griddled with red peppers and harissa paste – I didn't need to ask whether the traditional chilli condiment was home-made. As Rachid tore pieces from a loaf and handed them around I asked him about one of the pictures we had seen. A younger version of himself had beamed from one of the frames, holding a scroll. I asked him what he had studied.

'I graduated with an engineering degree, though I haven't used it. At first it upset my father.' I asked him why he didn't make use of it. 'Because I wanted for nothing more than what I grew up with.' He continued with a smile, 'My brothers and sisters now call me the 'happy one'.'

I thought of Fatima, should she achieve her wish one day, and remembered once thinking that the secret to happiness is not getting what you want, but wanting what you have.

Rachid's ploy that afternoon had been to fulfil one of the

principles of his religion and welcome strangers to his house to offer them food. Delighted at being able to help him (how selfless of us!), we gave him the remainder of the sweets and Philip offered him the hat he had been wearing as a memento. Rachid seemed delighted with it, though as we drove off I said this was probably also due to some form of spiritual imperative, in helping rid me of a companion wearing a straw boater.

We had neglected to ask Rachid about Volubilis. It was only ten miles away so he would have been able to advise us. Instead we asked a policeman at a checkpoint with a thumbs-up and a shouted 'Volubilis – bon?' He reciprocated. As he wasn't wearing glasses we decided it was worth the drive. We had started to enjoy this form of impromptu sightseeing and I wondered whether it could be applied anywhere. I thought of Nottingham and conceded a *Lonely Planet* guide might be advisable in some cases.

Volubilis was well signposted – so well, in fact, that all roads seemed to lead there. When we arrived we discovered that its Roman origins might have been the reason for this. Volubilis had been the westernmost outpost of the Roman Empire and an important regional administration centre. Although devastated by two massive earthquakes in the fourth and eighteenth centuries, and much plundered for its marble to build nearby Meknes, it is one of the best preserved set of Roman ruins in northern Africa. It became a UNESCO World Heritage site in 1997: however it was blissfully unencumbered with anything that suggested it had become so important.

We were the only ones in the dusty car park, an aged coach having departed as we entered. Before we had the opportunity to turn off the engine, another official name badge, prepared with a typewriter that had seen better years, was wafted under our noses. Once again a string of British celebrity names was uttered as a form of greeting, capped with the ubiquitous catchphrase of Del Boy from *Only Fools and Horses*. The association was apt as he had the shifty gait of a stolen-goods salesman aware that he might be under surveillance. There was a manned ticket booth at the entrance to the site, though our self-appointed guide took our money and paid on our behalf, explaining that that we didn't need to pay him for a tour unless we had enjoyed his commentary. This we certainly did, though maybe not in the way he meant.

The site was certainly worth the time to visit, as surely nowhere else could one more clearly see the layout of a Roman town without the adulteration born of subsequent construction. The arches and columns of some of the more significant structures had been partially rebuilt to give an impression of their grandeur, and the function of some of the rooms, now only framed by low stone walls, was given away by fine mosaics or features such as millstones. Our guide, Kasim, said one such millstone had been used for grinding grapes for wine. His tour would have been much appreciated by anyone hard of sight, though those able to read the information sheets tied to the short posts might easily conduct their own tour more accurately. A glance at the one near the millstone indicated the large pieces of basalt would indeed be too harsh for crushing grapes and were in fact for flour. This however didn't diminish our appreciation of his enthusiasm as he whisked us from point to point among the deserted ruins. If we loitered he could be heard somewhere ahead, his chirpy voice calling from some nook or other he considered of interest; with the sole intent, I suspect, of hastening our tour. I thought his enthusiasm had gone too far when I heard his voice from behind a wall ahead.

'Would you like to see penis?'

This had been directed at me as Philip was some way off doing a little filming. I considered myself unluckier than him with his earlier admirer. I called that I would rather not. He insisted that it was the largest example I would see in Morocco. I was about to say that there would be only one I would be seeing in Morocco, my own, when he emerged, thankfully still clothed.

'Call your friend with his camera; he would like to film it, yes?' No, I explained, probably not.

'It is famous in all Morocco and many women have come to worship it …' I can't say I wasn't a little envious, but I began to back away. It was when he added 'since third century BC' that I was reassured. I entered the room from which he had come. At the centre was indeed the largest phallus I'd be seeing in Morocco (at over half a metre long I can say this without shame), carved on a low granite plinth. 'This is the room of orgies,' he explained. 'Ladies would sit upon the pedestal when they were ready for the men.' He emphasised this with a somewhat unnecessary rhythmic motion of his hips and added, a little wistfully, that this only took place in Roman times.

We continued the latter part of the tour enjoying his florid commentary, by now unconcerned that it might differ from the official texts. We ended the tour next to the dozing ticket salesman and thanked Kasim, asking him how much his fee was. He replied, 'You give what you like, whatever you like my friend.' We handed over a note, twice the entry fee. 'But maybe you like to give more than that.' It seemed there was a price he had in mind. We went to and fro in the same vein for a minute or two. When we eventually refused to go higher he thanked us warmly, indicating we'd gone a long way past his target. There was an art to haggling and we still had a lot to learn.

Before we left we asked if there was somewhere locally

we could set the tent up. Again, the safety issue was raised. He suggested we stay at a hotel he knew very well in Moulay Idriss and gave us directions. It would be clean and was very nice. We would be treated well. We took him at his word, though as we later entered the town I wondered whether our safety had been his real concern.

From where we were standing Moulay Idriss could be seen nestled in a cleft in the hills some way along the valley. Idriss 1 had founded the town. He was the descendent of Muhammad who first brought Islam to the Maghreb countries in the late 700s. When he arrived, what remained of Volubilis didn't appeal and so the new settlement was created. Needless to say, it is a highly significant town, and, housing the tomb of its founder, a major pilgrimage site for Muslims. Contrary to our method of travelling without a guidebook, this I would have been happy to learn before we drove into town with a camera strapped to our bonnet.

As we climbed into the hills, the temperature dropped, but only enough to refresh the stale air in the car, the heat having taken its toll on the contents of our neglected coolbox. The wire leading to the remote camera lens flapped on the bonnet and the little monitor registered our progress among the olive groves as the splash of white housing clinging to the amber hillside grew before us. Any fool could capture the moment with a half decent camera here, we thought; and indeed, that's precisely what we were.

The first sign of life we saw in the hills, a man walking a donkey laden with sticks, added to the scene. We waved as had become the norm, but his face remained as stoic as the donkey's. Philip and I had been playing the waving game ever since we had arrived in Morocco, something my brother and I had begun in our youth when on holiday. When going somewhere new we would wave at fifty people and count the number we received back: a crude test of local friendliness

108

(a weekend in Berkshire had put an end to the game for some years). Morocco was now in first place on my all-time league table, narrowly beating Madeira (where the chief national pastime is sitting on doorsteps saluting traffic). The next response, a scowl from two women carrying water, was not enough to have us thinking something was amiss. The big clue came as we entered the town and people stared at us, as might a mourner seeing topless dancers in a funeral cortege. We dismantled the camera and stowed it out of sight.

This may have helped matters, but we were still observed with caution. As we entered the town's square I wondered whether this was simply because we had our own transport – all of the parking spaces were occupied by old Mercedes taxis and their drivers, about forty in all.

Unable to park, I left Philip with the car at the roadside and set off to find the hotel. A hand painted sign, suspiciously like the one that had guided us to Volubilis, pointed the way down a narrow flight of steps off the square. The high building sides cut out much of the last of the evening sun and the granite flagstones lent a chill to the air. Having put on something more than a tee shirt might have been advisable. At the foot of the steps another sign led me down an alleyway strung with washing high above. Sounds floated down from some of the open windows, but there was no one around at street level. At the next intersection I looked about for directions. A man leant out of a window, something in the half-light was familiar about him. He pointed down another alley and called, 'Hotel, that way', before disappearing. Pleased, though a little surprised by the unsolicited assistance, I followed his advice. As I walked on I became thankful for the signs, as much for the fact that they could guide me back to Philip as for leading me to the hotel. I imagined my companion by now surrounded by disgruntled taxi drivers. A few minutes later I was again unsure which direction to take when a child touched my arm from behind, causing me to start. 'Looking for a hotel? Come, this way.' Assuming there could be no other reason why he would think I might be here, I let him guide me a final few turns before he deposited me in front of an open doorway. He disappeared down an alley, not leaving me time to thank him. Voices emanated from the end of a dark hallway, yet there seemed to be no reception, nor any other sign that this was a hotel at all. I stood for a moment and someone approached from within, the tap-tap of a walking cane on the floor preceding a face from the gloom. 'You need a hotel,' the old lady's wavering voice uttering a statement rather than a question. Something in her demeanour suggested that she hadn't completed the full term at hotel school and an unnerving familiarity in her features influenced my answer: 'No, I'm looking for a taxi, which way do I need to go?' She eyed me suspiciously as if she knew I was lying then simply jerked her thumb back the way I'd come. Retracing my route in, I reached Philip easily and found him with a taxi driver, but rather than anything sinister, they were in good-natured conversation. Philip asked what the hotel was like and I shook my head. The taxi driver told us there was no hotel in Moulay Idriss, but there was a good one very near Volubilis, overlooking the ruins from the hills. He thought to himself for a while and then asked whether we had already been there, as the only other people he'd ever met looking for a hotel in Moulay Idriss had just visited the ruins.

I'm still unsure whether it was our dress that made us feel out of place in the town (I later read that bare arms on a male can be viewed as inappropriate in holy places). It could have been the camera of course, or maybe a combination, though I have subsequently learnt there is a myth surrounding Moulay Idriss that says visitors are intentionally made to feel unwelcome, after all, it was prohibited for non-Muslims to sleep in the town up until 2007. However, as I don't wish to perpetuate a myth due to our insensitivity, I'll let you make up your own mind.

The receptionist at Hotel Volubilis seemed delighted as she photocopied our passports at check-in.

'Welcome, welcome, Prince Charles!' As this was not uttered by a fixer or tour guide I wasn't sure whether this was the now familiar greeting intended to endear, or whether she thought either of us was indeed the monarch-in-waiting. I wondered whether to go with it and hope for an upgrade, but she pointed to a framed photograph of the Prince shaking hands with the manager of the establishment. She told us he had visited in 2001, with his friend Tony Blair. As the latter wasn't in shot (and the thought of the two holidaying together stretched the imagination) perhaps the then prime minister had not been there at all, but there could be no doubt that Charles had – even Disney would have trouble creating a computer-generated shot this convincing. At first I wondered why royalty might come to stay at all, then I considered the only alternative accommodation for anyone wishing to visit the historical site – though the thought of Kasim directing the heir to the throne and his entourage to what I now believe was his mother's house, was one to savour.

Built on an outcrop at the top of a ridge above Volubilis, the hotel's location had sold it to us before we'd entered. It commanded a view of the ruins and, beyond the valley floor, the Atlas foothills. It was also empty, in itself worth another star rating in my opinion. Not that I particularly dislike sharing hotels with others, but it's fun occasionally to be the sole focus of those about you, albeit just for an evening – unlike the future monarch, who has to experience it daily.

Having checked in, we made our way to the hotel's most

prominent feature, a terrace overlooking the columns and arches, now silhouetted in the sunset. We ordered a bottle of Castel's Carignan Gris to round the day off where it had started, and its redcurrant and herb aromas mingled with those of cactus and dried scrub carried up from beneath the terrace. There was nothing to disturb the sense of tranquillity save for the occasional soft put-put of a distant scooter.

We had passed nearly an hour writing up notes and viewing film when a bloodcurdling scream came from a little way down the hill, amplified by the rocks. Startled, we looked to one another, thinking someone was being attacked. It came again, this time the shriek longer and more tortured. Showing my concern, I looked to our waiter who was wiping down a nearby table. He smiled politely as it came again, indicating we shouldn't worry and clasped his hands together before walking off. Did this mean we should pray for the individual in question and do nothing? We were incensed at his lack of concern. We listened out, thinking should we hear it again we would report it to someone in authority. When, some moments later, the cry came once more, this time even more impassioned, we knew we should act. The reception was deserted when we arrived. We rang the bell and were presently attended to by our waiter, who, not speaking French, seemed confused and responded in the same casual manner as before. We tried looking for another staff member, without success, then went back to the balcony and waited to discern from where the scream had come. We heard nothing more and made our way to our room for the night. I thought about the chilling nature of the cry as I dozed off and was pleased we hadn't camped: a satisfaction assisted by the fact that I had just brushed my teeth in Prince Charles's sink.

The following morning brought an early start for our appointment at the aptly named Volubilia, a Franco Moroccan winery that had used the ancient site as inspiration for its name.

As we handed our keys to our cheery receptionist the scream rang out again. Had the man been tortured all night? I looked to the woman and she mimicked the waiter from the night before, and added, 'That is our Imam, sir. His megaphone has been stolen, so he has to call people to prayer without it.

We had become used to the eerie wailing chants providing aural texture to our setting, though, it seemed, whilst maybe as effective, they lost a certain level of charm without assisted amplification.

The Volubilia estate was back across the valley in the mountains. From where we'd been sitting at breakfast I calculated it would only take half an hour to traverse the empty plain. However I had not accounted for unexpected traffic. (I console myself that this is something one can never do, otherwise it becomes expected traffic, which makes the whole process of accounting for it much easier.)

We could see Moulay Idriss receding in the rear view mirror as we set off, the morning sun catching the white and lifting the townscape from the hillside. Although we considered our start early, the fields had been worked since first light. The mules and donkeys, along with their masters, all seemed to have permanent accommodation in their plots: the reed dwellings completing a scene that would barely have altered in centuries. This was not a setting to expect the modern scourge of road rage.

I consider myself a calm individual at the wheel (and not just in contrast to my passengers). It has been some time since I've risen to the challenge of a revved engine at a set of lights, or felt my blood pressure rise in a traffic jam, though there are times when a driver can be pushed too far. I still can't imagine why a mobile phone company (let alone the company responsible for Philip's phone) should choose to advertise their new wafer-thin 3G handset to the farmers of northern Morocco. I'm sure that smallholders wresting vegetables from the ground are worthy individuals and probably an untapped market, but to spend money painting eight brand new cars with advertising, and have them slowly parade past the fields seemed out of place, cruel even.

Although I find irritating any moving vehicle whose sole function is advertising, my heart rate had barely wavered as I overtook the dawdling convoy. Before I had time to complete the manoeuvre however, a cart pulled out into the road before us. I signalled to pull back in but the cars closed ranks beside me. My options were to: have a horse join me in the driver's seat, or forcibly cut in, so I chose the latter. This caused unimagined chaos. I was now punctuating the message written across their vehicles. Being in Arabic, I'm unsure what it said, though I assumed it was now something rude, such was their desire to regroup. Their pride now dented, the drivers behind us passed either side at speed and re-formed. It was a manoeuvre of choreographed beauty and worthy of praise from any Tunisian driving instructor. Philip had seemed unflustered by the encounter so far, but I could sense his concern at my next move.

Retreating some way to allow space to build momentum, I then floored the accelerator and threw them a dummy. I made to overtake, and, as they predictably rippled out to block my progress, I cut to the inside, passing seven of them before they swung back in. I had only one to overtake, though my wing mirrors were full of what seemed to be a dismembered transformer from a sci-fi movie fervently regrouping to attack. I managed to maintain our advantage as

114

we neared the foot of a hill, using more shoulder than tarmac, then mounted a final assault on the weaving front man.

To watch this from a distance (as was being done via a set of binoculars) must have provided quite a distraction to a quiet morning. At the time I thought myself worthy of congratulation for my stance against globalised advertising, but this was not to be the attitude of the police at the roadblock ahead.

I passed the leader with a brinkmanship that informed us both I was the marginally more insane and, once the little convoy was again in unison, the drivers seemed content to slow to their original pace. Being late, I'd maintained my momentum: probably another of the reasons I was asked to stop and step out of the vehicle, just as eight smug faces passed though the checkpoint unhindered. The policeman took some time explaining each of the laws I'd infringed (I hadn't been aware that running over cacti was an offence) and he listed the penalties. Knowing that showing sufficient deference before the law can mitigate the outcome, I chose not to ask why he wasn't out catching real criminals and simply nodded and looked apologetic. He peered into the Land Rover and eyed Philip, then asked us what we had in the trunks. He seemed contented by the reply (we had casually omitted the filming equipment) and asked what the car's fuel consumption was. Fearing this could be a further infringement, I generously added a few miles to the car's true economy. He nodded thoughtfully and looked impressed, explaining that his did far less. I knew we were on safer ground when he asked to look at the engine, though didn't feel it was yet time to invoke the names of famous football players. I tried to answer his questions about the car in the manner of a fellow enthusiast, but, as much as I harked back to when I bought it, I wasn't sure if it was a 'straight six' or a 'V something'. He frowned momentarily, possibly considering whether I'd stolen it, before clasping my hand and welcoming us to Morocco. We were free to go. I had learned that the bond of the Land Rover fraternity ran deeper than the wave I received from fellow drivers. Instead of embarrassedly raising a finger in response, I would now wave back with gusto.

* * *

Imagine you are a gymnast. You've trained for many years and have made Olympic standard. Once at the Games you are asked to compete also at archery and you achieve a gold. Awards and accolades lined the wall at Volubilia, but not for wine; instead it seemed that we'd arrived at the world's finest producer of olives for oil.

In keeping with most of those involved in joint ventures, when in 2001 Gérard Gribelin and Philippe Gervoson, two highly respected Bordeaux winemakers, signed up to make wine in Morocco, they inherited olive groves as part of the deal. This enables wineries to be run as an agribusiness, something that helps make the occasionally contentious subject of winemaking more acceptable. In 2006 the Italian olive oil bible, *Extravirgine*, awarded the oil from their olives the title 'best in the world', from an entry of 3000. As Gérard's son, Christophe (now in charge) and the winemaker, Philippe Lespy (formerly of Château Lafite), led us into the vineyard, they described this as a happy accident, but as we progressed I considered it was more down to passion and attention to detail in one field being successfully applied to another.

'There is no secret to good olive oil, as there is no secret to good wine,' Philippe explained with a boyish enthusiasm that left no space for boast. He went on to explain that if you have a good climate and soil all you need is respect for the plant. He then moved from grapevine to grapevine, pointing out their differences and how they were treated as individuals. He allowed them, within limits, their own development patterns 'as if they are children'. I said that children took some looking after and 240,000 would need an inordinate amount of attention. He explained that manpower here, unlike in countries with a higher concentration of vineyards, was easier to come by. Also, people adapted to his way of working, and not being consumers of wine in no way diminished the pride in their work. I suppose there can be fine craftsmen who don't wish to be on the receiving end of their expertise – surgeons for instance.

I had only seen this level of attention at some of the world's top vineyards, and many of those didn't even go as far. Each vine was pruned according to what was best for it and each received enough water for its own needs. Philippe explained that he wanted to stress each vine to maximise its development (not enough stress leading to weakly flavoured grapes), enabling it to produce the right quantity of grapes with as much flavour as possible. He also explained that despite his background at one of the finest vineyards in Bordeaux, he couldn't afford to think in French; instead he had to think in Moroccan if he were to make the best wine possible. 'In France much of the work in the vineyard involves practices that ensure we get good ripeness; here we have to slow the ripening process to enable flavour to develop in the grapes.' To do this they were using techniques such as shading the grapes with leaf cover and planting in a way that reduces the amount of sun that gets to them: practices commonplace in Australia. Having worked in Western Australia's Swan Valley, I mentioned the association, and that the late springtime temperatures that morning would be similar to those around Perth in the same season there. Christophe explained that at 800 metres above

117

sea level, the site was chosen as it was cooler than other vineyard areas and had a big swing in temperature between day and night, another factor helping to slow the ripening process and allow flavour to fully develop.

Something then caught my eye. It lifted my heartbeat and distracted my attention. I moved away from the group.

Later, reviewing the film Philip had taken that morning, I could see Christophe and Philippe smiling as they watched me peer at an adjacent plot, fully aware of what I had spotted. Having a similar regard for soil, they were pleased I'd noticed there were parts of the vineyard that had very similar characteristics to those of Bordeaux. The type of soil, loose brown earth sifted between smooth stones, like a muddy pebble beach, was not the preserve of Bordeaux either; some of the best vineyards of Chile and Spain, amongst others, are similar.

It seemed that the ideal combination for successful winemaking was complete: here was the passion, the climate and the soils; I had proof that Morocco indeed had the potential to make truly fine wines, but would these wines reach the same heady heights that Volubilia's olive oil had?

In their offices we got off to a very good start with a lovely Volubilia Gris (gris being the category, popular in northern Africa, lighter in hue than the standard rosé). This was made from a blend of the increasingly fashionable Mourvèdre and Tempranillo (the latter responsible for Rioja). It combined the best of both on the nose, the savoury herb whiff of the former with the cherry jam of the latter. It was crisper and fresher than any example of the style I'd yet tasted and I asked how much acidity had been added to achieve this. It is widely accepted that in the hottest of climates it is essential to add acidity back into the wine, as much is lost on the vine as the grape ripens (conversely, cooler climates can struggle to lose it sufficiently). Philippe

118

looked proudly at me as he had taken my comment as a compliment. He explained the acidity was natural as they manage to retain it in the vineyard by protecting the grapes against excessive heat. I hadn't come across many Australian wineries that achieved this. There was a mouth-watering rosé too, from the unusual Caladoc and Marselan grapes. Next came an attention-grabbing but elegant Chardonnay, the very best of what most Californian Chardonnay used to be before most tried to emulate Burgundy and got lighter. It was warm and tropical with notes of ripe dessert apple, sweet custard, green almonds and dried quince but had a crisp feel in the mouth thanks to the acidity. I thought it would fare well against some considerably more expensive US examples.

Next up were the reds, and these followed in the same impressive manner, surprising me with their elegance and range of aromas. Commenting on the latter, I was told they were able to preserve some of the more delicate aromas often lost at harvest by adding dry-ice to the buckets into which they were picked, helping to avoid oxidation: novel, and expensive no doubt. The range was topped, as seemed to be the way, by a Syrah, from their new Epicuria range. With good wines, the pen flows easily and I had just finished a shopping list of flavours including fleshy plums, truffle, game, ginger and angelica (and had drawn a smiley face) when I asked if they had any older examples of the wine to see how it would develop. 'This is our first year.' The vines were only four years old when this was made. Impressive wines indeed from such young vines.

The verdict? Would their best wine outshine the best in the world as their oil had? No, that would be too much to ask of a new vineyard. Their range would certainly sit well alongside many more expensive wines, but the finest wines in the world are, without exception, those that have all that Volubilia has (good climate, good soil and an intelligent approach to vine growing); but the very best have older vines and time enough to understand how to get the most from them. I have no doubt however, that as these vines age, and if the same respect is paid to them in future, they will yield quality to truly put Morocco on the fine wine map.

Our two-hour morning appointment had morphed into a full day with the pair, capped by an outdoor lunch that saw the winery workers clocking off before we'd had coffee. A feature of the lunch had been some 2007 Syrah from cask, which was even more complex than the 2006, boding well for the future. It was so good, in fact, that I neglected to make any notes on it, except a mental one to taste it again sometime. We declined a grappa (as our faces were flushed enough, though I assured Philip mine was due to the sun) and we asked if there was anywhere interesting nearby to spend the evening. The blank looks and hesitation preceding the suggestion should have told us that it might not have been worth following up. They said there was a village further into the mountains, alpine in nature, which had a reputation for being a winter escape for those in Meknes. Relishing the prospect of cooler climes – the day having hit and maintained a constant 30 degrees – we accepted a generous gift of three magnums of Volubilia Gris and set off into the hills.

We were now at the furthest point west in the Atlas Mountains, having skirted the middle portion by avoiding Algeria. As we climbed I thought about what lay in between and knew there should be the same favourable conditions for great wines there. Yet I wondered whether strict state control on the now vastly diminished Algerian industry would allow the potential to blossom in the same way it was beginning to in Morocco.

The agriculture in the fertile valleys around Volubilia

gave way to dry pasture as we gained altitude, which in turn changed to scrub oak. The forest floor was littered with smooth boulders dappled in sunlight, and birds of prey circled above – though this time Philip chose not to film them, the association still too painful.

We spotted a lone figure selling something ahead. It again seemed clear that a niche in Morocco exists for anyone wishing to set up a marketing course for roadside salesmen – how on earth did the man think he could make money by selling his produce in such an unfrequented spot?

'Is he selling honey?' asked Philip.

'Looks like it.'

'Let's stop.'

'Are there any bees?'

'Don't think so.'

'Fine, let's.'

The man lifted the wide brimmed hat from the bridge of his nose and raised himself from the grassy bank (I knew it, a lifestyle business). He smiled and raised his eyebrows, as if wondering why we'd stopped. He didn't speak French, so Philip pointed to his stack of large plastic jars, which, telling by the labelling, had once contained mayonnaise. A ray of sun cut through the stack, giving the amber honey a luminescence that made it all the more appealing. He gestured to the man to ask how much for a jar. He gave us a figure, which we considered value indeed – probably less than a tenth that of the processed stuff made by the sweat shops in England (there's no fair trade for bees!). Philip said thank you, but before he could get to his money, the man reduced his price. Philip tried to explain that the original price was fair, but the man again lowered his fee in a manner that indicated that it was his final offer. He reduced it again as Philip tried to reassure him. He now looked genuinely distressed – my friend was certainly grinding him down! We were in danger of not getting any honey at all when Philip next spoke – the man walked away, the deal off. Philip took out the original amount and walked up to him using the power of mime to indicate we would pay him that. We were now contented owners of three litres of mountain honey and he looked genuinely pleased that we might pay his asking price. There is a feeling felt by many from richer countries that they are being ripped off if they don't grind down a seller to the same level a local might. That afternoon we thought that it wasn't such a bad thing to consider something's worth to us, rather than its value to a local, who most likely does not have the same expendable income. In Fes this maxim was to be tested beyond breaking point, turning us once again into hard-bitten avaricious capitalists.

We dipped a finger into the warm viscous liquid as we drove and as it was so good we pulled out some bread to have with it. It was as interesting to smell as good wine, grassy aromas mingled with more floral notes, all overlaid with a tinge of caramelisation lent by its time in the sun.

I don't know if there's ever been an investigation conducted into honey's incendiary effects on the contents of a stomach subjected to rich foods, and possibly unsanitary water, but I was about to be a prime case study.

Some minutes later, having driven through the upper tree-line into alpine pasture, we were humming along to 'You're The First, The Last, My Everything', when I felt the desperate urge to stop; but with such speed that Barry White skipped a track on the CD. I shall spare you the details of the next few moments, though I was left a considerably lighter man, and one in some discomfort, when I returned from behind an oak tree. With Philip now driving at an increased speed we made our way to what we hoped was an alpine idyll with loos. The roofline that greeted us as we crested a ridge didn't disappoint, the pitched gables meeting our expectations. From a distance the cluster of chalet buildings had a cool air of calm, giving a modicum of relief to my situation. Further respite was forthcoming when we saw a sign for a hotel. There was no thought now of sleeping in the roof-tent. I wanted the comfort of a bed from which a sink and loo could be reached without what, in my predicament, would feel like descending the north face of the Eiger.

The town appeared well planned and the wide boulevards beautifully tended. We later found out that the French were responsible for the planning – when building it as a cool summer retreat for its administration of the protectorate – though we couldn't guess who was now taking care of the neatly clipped grass and blooming shrub life, as the town was deserted.

We'd quickly reached the far side of the compact municipality, and were waiting to turn into the hotel's grounds, when we were overtaken by an army personnel carrier packed with soldiers swaddled in layers of clothing that would have us dying of heat exhaustion. They parked up before us, though I leapt from the car and rushed into the reception (despite fear of a further episode) keen not to be deprived of a bed. I made it in advance of the disembarking troops, and, bent double, triumphantly thrust my passport into the hands of the receptionist. It was promptly handed back. The hotel had been block booked by the military for local manoeuvres. Having noticed the tent box on the vehicle, the receptionist suggested there was a compound where we could camp nearby and said we would be quite safe there. 'There's nobody in town except the army,' she laughed. I failed to see the humour in her point on two counts: firstly, the lack of accommodation: and secondly, the sullen demeanour of the men now queuing behind me did not suggest they were here for our benefit. I passed them on the way out with the airy gait of someone who has not just tried to beat them to a bedroom – not an easy feat with a colon in the throes of wild fermentation. Philip, having witnessed the scene, asked what I would like to do. I said it was what I wanted to stop doing that most preoccupied me, and rushed back into the hotel. Once back out Philip gave me our options: it was to be the compound, or a hotel in Meknes. The latter, now fifty miles away, was where we were due for a meeting late the following morning. The thought of the journey alone caused rumblings below, so I suggested we try camping.

From outside, the compound held promise, as, due to an eight-foot wall, we couldn't see inside. From there things deteriorated. The entry barrier lay broken across the entrance, suggesting, along with foot-high grass in every plot, that it hadn't been used for some time – the length of which was indicated by the only other car inside: an abandoned VW camper, florally decorated in emulsion that seemed to have withstood the decades better than the vehicle itself.

I spotted a loo-block. My digestive system somewhat optimistically drew me towards it, but at a distance of five metres I was having second thoughts. The indication of gender was, ironically, a silhouette of an Edwardian gentleman with top hat and cane. I pictured a queue of such figures, prostrate outside the viciously odorous block, flailing their canes in a death rattle. The compound, we concluded, would not make it high on a list of World Health Organization's 'places to recover from gastric upheaval', so we made our way out.

As we did, I was struck by a sense of déjà vu, though at first I couldn't put my finger on it. A man was now sitting by the entrance. He approached and told us the fee for staying for the evening. Even I was able to decline his offer and we drove off. As Philip turned into the road I looked to my wing mirror and saw him light a cigarette, in the same easy manner as when he'd been standing in the queue at the hotel. Now in mufti, his uniform would no doubt be hanging in a warm room.

We drove to Meknes in stages punctuated by impromptu stops, to the rather more therapeutic surroundings of the oddly named Hotel Zaki. I spent many hours that night staring at the name etched into the loo-roll holder, and couldn't help but be struck by the only phonetic anagram the name contained.

* * *

'Dr Gimblett I presume?'

In my somewhat diminished state – leaning next to our vehicle outside the hotel the following morning – it took some moments to recognise this as humorous reference to British exploration. I suppose my mode of dress that day hadn't been selected with assimilation to Islamic culture in mind – khaki shorts and Panama hats not being something we'd encountered a great deal.

Jean Pierre, our host for the morning, looked expectantly as I searched for a response. He had just arrived with his personal assistant, Fadoua, an elegant young woman with sphinx-like features. Before he'd even spoken I already liked Jean Pierre. I don't believe that first impressions are everything, though the twinkle in his eye, and a grin as broad as his sturdy shoulders, were enough to leave anyone with the impression that this was a genial man. My rejoinder, whilst not witty, or indeed academically accurate, revealed he had the right man.

'Yes.'

Philip quickly introduced himself and moved the conversation along nicely, thanking Jean Pierre for seeing us.

I mentioned the reason for my being a little subdued and asked if we mightn't stray too far from some form of amenity during the course of our visit. Sympathy was forthcoming from Fadoua, which from someone so glamorous rarely fails to comfort. She went as far as apologising for the hygiene on behalf of wherever I'd picked up the bug, and seemed quite genuine in saying so. The fault was with my antibodies I explained, since we are too cosseted in the UK and it was just my system adjusting. My sentiment was not just politeness in the presence of an attractive woman; I do feel we are sometimes a little too keen on eradicating all bacteria in our foods in Northern Europe and it may not always be as good for us as the shiny surfaces in the adverts suggest.

As we followed the pair to the winery in their car, we were mesmerised by the silhouette of Jean Pierre's gestures as he spoke. Wildly oscillating, his hands were never near the steering wheel at the same time unless they occasionally came together in a last-minute attempt to avoid livestock or passers by. He had also apparently developed the ability to see through his left ear, such was the attention paid to his attractive passenger.

We shortly arrived at a large sandstone arch and set of wrought iron gates some miles to the south of Meknes: the entrance to Morocco's only wine Château, Château Roslane. Although the distinction has about as much official meaning in Morocco as it has in France (the building was an elegant Moroccan villa painted in soft earth pastels), it was more deserving of the title than a fair proportion of the allotment sheds laying claim to it in Bordeaux. Almost symmetrical palm trees shaded the gardens about the property, vividly coloured lavender bushes blossoming at their feet. The grass seemed to have been clipped with the assistance of a spirit level and an air of order pervaded every corner. This continued as we were led into the immaculate winery.

Everything had its place and between those places was deliberate space, giving the inactive building a sense of peaceful proportion that could not fail to temper the atmosphere at the normally frenetic harvest time. No expense had been spared on equipment, though not all of it designed specifically to replace manual labour, as is the way in many wineries, but instead to work in harmony with it to get the best out of the wine. Stacks of small picking baskets stood silently waiting for the vintage, next to rows of vibrating sorting tables that would take upwards of twenty labourers to operate. Jean Pierre said that bunches were picked into small containers to avoid premature crushing and preserve quality, and that individual grapes were sorted rigorously by hand to eliminate poorer ones. I mentioned that they were fortunate to have a good source of inexpensive labour. He explained that one of the company's directors had recently conducted research into mechanising the harvesting and eliminating costs in the winery and it was found that considerable savings could still be made, despite a readily available workforce. He said that when the research was presented to the owner, Brahim Zniber, it was dismissed as out of the question. He had asked what would become of the families of the unemployed workers.

This was not the sentiment of a man with a communist ethic, but that of the most successful businessman in Morocco, and a man, judging by the genuine admiration felt by our hosts that morning, who is much loved by his staff. Brahim Zniber is now the third richest man in Morocco and the owner of over thirty businesses, including insurance, banking and the Moroccan Coca-Cola franchise. He started with nothing, and his wine business (Celliers de Meknes, of which Château Roslane is the flagship estate) was his first passion. He is the man responsible for Morocco's wine resurgence, pushing for world recognition not only for his wines, but also official quality designations for the regions from which they come. This promotion has not always sat well with the country's uneasy, and often paradoxical, relationship with the grape. As a trade figurehead, he was singled out for strong criticism in the national press after a wine festival was held in Meknes in 2007. The festival was seen as diminishing Islam within Morocco. It was as much that the festival was held on a Friday (the day of prayer, one step away from holding it within Ramadan) as that it was seen to be overt promotion of wine, there being severe restrictions on its advertising.

There are those who point to parts of the Koran that are apparently permissive of wine consumption: 'We give you the fruit of the palm and vine, from which you derive intoxicants and wholesome food' (Sura 16:69). There are more who can back their claims that it preaches abstinence: 'Satan seeks to stir up enmity and hatred among you by means of wine and gambling and keep you from Allah and your prayers, will you not abstain from them?' (Sura 5:91). The reality in Morocco is that a sizeable minority choose their own interpretation where wine is concerned (watching shoppers at a hypermarket is enough to convince you of that) without it affecting other aspects of their faith.

As we sat to a tasting, I asked who would be taking over from Mr Zniber when he retired, as, although he looked a man of sixty, he was actually in his eighties. 'One of his four hundred children.' Jean Pierre smiled and said that twelve are Mr Zniber's own, seven were adopted, and the rest are in his orphanages, which he founded as part of his faith.

I considered that in any faith, any devil to be found will be within the detail, rather than the sentiment.

It was clear when tasting Mr Zniber's wines that the thought and investment put into Château Roslane was being rewarded with abundance. The range was good, particularly the flagship red and white under the Château Roslane label.

After having left Jean Pierre and Fadoua, we had scoured the map for another spot of interest. We hadn't needed a guidebook to tell us that Fes might fit the bill, such was its renown – though if pressed at the time I would probably have said little other than it was old and possibly the birthplace of the hat, as they also spell it with a 'z'. (However, I was wrong about this connection, as the bright red headpiece originated in Turkey as military wear and was discontinued in that form, unsurprisingly, after the invention of the gun.) We had driven the sixty kilometres from Meknes and were nearing the city without a coherent plan.

'You need camping?'
   'No thank you.'
   'Hotel?'
   'No, thank you.'
   'Tour guide?'
   'No.'
   'Laundry?'
   'No!'
   'Food, beer, cup of tea?' The features on the thickly lined face that had thrust itself somewhat athletically through the car window suggested surely we needed one of these things.
   'No, we're going to buy some wine, and we are going to buy it over there,' I said with finality, pointing to the supermarket beyond the junction.
   'Excellent, I wait for you to buy the wine, then I show you camping!'
   'No!'
   'Hotel …' The lights had changed and I pulled away with acceleration normally reserved for Grand Prix drivers. A

glance behind us indicated that the man had a level of tenacity so far unencountered; and a scooter. Philip looked faintly resigned as I increased speed and we passed the entrance to the supermarket. The figure pursuing on the ancient Vespa was unable to respond in kind, and shrank to a speck as we ran the next two sets of lights and sped on.

'Is he still behind?' I asked after some minutes.

'I hardly think so. The supermarket will be closing in ten minutes; we'll have to make do with warm rosé.'

'We can get back in time,' I said, 'by going cross country!' Maybe it was some residual sympathy after my food poisoning episode that allowed Philip to indulge my cunning plan without comment. He simply nodded as I turned off, and we made our way back obscured by the low buildings and bushes lining the road.

The car park was all but deserted and a worker was bringing in trolleys for the night when we arrived with a minute to spare. This didn't stop the assistant in the wine section spending a considerable amount of time explaining their offer to me, something I was grateful for, though I was aware that Philip might be getting impatient outside. As I selected some bottles we had not yet tasted, the young lady told me about them, including details on methods of production and history. I made some notes and she seemed delighted to share her knowledge. When I asked which her favourite was, she rather inevitably replied that she didn't drink wine. I considered that her levels of knowledge and consumption were both the direct inverse of those exhibited by the staff at our supermarket in Haslemere.

Pleased with the weight of my burgeoning box, I thanked the store manager patiently waiting by the door to lock up, and made my way back to the car – to a scene that pleased me rather less than it seemed to be pleasing Philip. He was in deep conversation with our pursuer and relations had developed to a level where they were sharing a joke. I unkindly wondered whether the man had already asked Philip if he needed a cleaner.

I approached the pair and looked over to the scooter, wondering where the man positioned his on-board radar. Philip introduced me to Mohammed, saying that he had kindly offered to show us somewhere to camp. The moment the man's head was turned I flashed Philip a forcefully questioning look, implying that we'd likely be murdered in our beds.

Under a faded plastic anorak Mohammed wore a stiff smock (whose rigidity I doubted was down to fresh starch) and on his head sat a baseball cap, incongruous not because it advertised whisky, but because it threw his shock of tight curls out to each side, leaving him looking like Mickey Mouse in silhouette. He had an easy smile and a gentle way of moving that I thought far too studied to be trusted. This was a shrewd man wishing to appear less so, I thought. However, we packed the wine away and followed the buzzing scooter into the city.

'And what time will the factory re-open, Mohammed?' asked Philip. Even he wasn't convinced that the concrete plot we were now standing on was widely accepted as being a campsite. I suggested to Philip that we get back into the car and go to the hotel we'd just passed.

'That hotel is bad for you! Let me take you to a luxury one, half the price of the one with bad bugs (it could have been bed bugs). My friend, he will give you the best room.' I thought of again using velocity to put distance between us but felt the task inadvisable in such a built-up place. He then led us through an area resembling suburban Paris – this was looking better I thought – but on to a street to shame downtown Calcutta. The hotel sign was missing its 't' (or could it have been a 'v', I thought, as we looked on). A chef sat on the front step, his bloody apron collecting the ash from his dangling cigarette. A scrawny cat joined him from within the hotel and sat on his lap. Mohammed looked at us.

'OK, I understand. I find you nice one in Fes.' I said surely we were in Fes? He shook his head and said this was French Fes and then asked us to follow him. I once again thought to lose him but the roadsides were still too busy, so simply resigned myself to following.

We passed down the last few blocks of this particular Fes, with its boulevards, plane trees and relatively orderly traffic system, and through a narrow sandstone arch, into an entirely different world: that of Fes el Bali, the original city. We guessed this at the time, though we knew little else, except that Idriss 1, the founder of Moulay Idriss, had built it. There was little to put us in mind of the medina's smaller cousin however as we were shadowed by laughing children and the beaming faces of residents leaning from their balconies. These changed from smiles of welcome to those of genuine admiration as the streets began to narrow and we manoeuvred the vehicle further into the medina. Mohammed stopped and waited at some junctions as we performed the series of delicate turns required to continue, though as often he was happy to disappear ahead, content no doubt in the knowledge that we were now his.

I tooted the horn and got out, because, even after retracting the wing mirrors, we could go no further. Mohammed appeared from around a corner he'd clearly expected us to navigate and reversed his scooter back to the car. I explained this was as far as we could go; we would have to go back – a challenge I was not relishing. He looked thoughtful for a moment.

'This is not a problem. We are here!' he said with a flourish.

He dismounted and walked over to a studded wooden

door, then knocked. He looked back at us and smiled, possibly aware of my suspicion. A man in a pale blue jallaba laced with silver filigree greeted our self-appointed guide with the studied look of one opening the door to a salesman, confirming my doubts. They spoke for some moments and nodded in agreement. Mohammed beckoned us over and explained that it was a lovely hotel and his friend would welcome us. I looked back to the car. Mohammed said that it would be safe where it was. I thought I'd welcome anyone else having a go at extracting it from this maze, even if it meant me having to somehow retrieve it later.

Once inside, our names were duly taken on a small pad, though for the first time in the trip our passports were waved away when presented. We were told that the man would prepare a room while we had a cup of tea, and we were whisked off before having time to discuss those things that most would consider practical or wise, such as the nature of the room or its price. I looked at my friend's trusting observation of the ornate tiles and family pictures as we passed down the hall, and realised that I would need to look after us both here. We passed from the gloom into a bright atrium that reached up through five floors, flowering plants hanging from the sills on all sides. A wooden table, decorated with fine bone and shell marquetry, sat with a silver pot and two cups already on its surface.

'Please do not sit!'

I raised myself with a start, thankful that I hadn't quite made contact with the stitched leather seat. Our host smiled to reassure me and asked if we would prefer to have our tea on the roof. I was going to say it was delightful where we were but Mohammed looked to indicate that our host might take offence should we decline his offer. We made our way up an irregular set of steps to the side of the atrium and past a number of closed doors, one of which I supposed might be our bedroom. Having an unconquered sense of vertigo, I was not relishing the prospect of being perched on a ledge five floors above the cobbles, but I needn't have worried. A wide veranda, thankfully bordered by a sturdy wrought iron balustrade, ran around the top of the atrium. We were shown to a table shaded by the leaves of a potted palm. The view immediately made me grateful for Philip's trusting nature. The terrace, a good two stories higher than any of the buildings sweeping down into the valley below, seemed the ideal spot from which to survey the ancient medina and its environs. Houses and streets fanned out for miles, as asymmetrical as crazed porcelain, spilling up the lower slopes of mountains either side. We were held in wonder as we gazed upon the intricate patterns of life unfolding below: beasts of burden working their way along impossibly narrow alleys, tea being taken by families on other rooftops, commerce on street corners, and above it all the lilting chants of the mosques. The smells of life in the warm city rose to greet us too, some cookery derived and pleasant, others more organic and less so, though none the less intriguing for it.

As the tea was poured, Mohammed said that we should have dinner in the city and that he had something we should see. My suspicious nature alerting me that at best it might be something he wished us to buy, and at worst I daren't guess, I said that we would be fine to visit the city alone. Mohammed smiled and asked what our plans were for the next day. I omitted the possibility of spending time with a movie star, but explained we were visiting a vineyard back towards Meknes.

'There are 9,400 streets in Fes. I have friend who lives here and still gets lost for days. I help to find him sometimes.' He continued to emphasise the unlikelihood of us making our meeting the next morning should we go it alone. Then, spurred on by the resigned look on my face, he said, 'I meet you in one hour.'

Mohammed turned up twenty minutes later as we were still drinking our tea: he didn't trust me! Seeing that we'd finished the little tray of pastries, laced with so much sugar that it doubled their weight, he asked if we were ready to go. We asked to see the room first and we were shown it on our way down. It was perfectly acceptable, rather better than we might have hoped. We then asked if there was anywhere safer for the car, as the storage boxes were unsecured. 'My friend, he will look after it,' said Mohammed. As we left the building I was a little taken aback to see an old man in a Berber smock sitting on the roof rack smoking a cigarette. His lazy salute and toothy smile, whilst not enough to put me fully at ease, left me unwilling to argue and we followed Mohammed into the city.

In the immediate vicinity the streets were bereft of the life we'd seen further into the city from above. Mohammed led us in silence, speaking only if we asked a question. I began to make mental note of our progress, though gave up after losing count of the number of turns we'd made: the moon was somewhere to the left now, though it had charted all points of the compass already. My sense of smell became more acute as dusk set in, gaining in importance as light faded, and because there was more to smell as we began to encounter life. The fresh waft of laundry being hung above mingled incongruously with the funk of a donkey carrying strings of dried chilli. Aromas of seared meat and charred vegetables from people's kitchens were soon overpowered by those from piles of freshly ground cardamom and other spices being sold from open windows, the confected scents from a soap-maker in turn usurping these. The colours of dyed silks breaking through the gloom soon vied with the aromas. As we moved on, shawls, carpets and leatherwear competed for our attention, their

135

craftsmanship leaving them hard to ignore. This was not a market but a way of existence, the open hatches leading directly into people's homes and lives. Above, friends conducted conversations from opposite balconies. The crooked walls leaning in to bring them closer were only held apart by pine joists, most of which were doubling as supports for drying clothes or vegetables. Tiny doorways gave glimpses of spaces beyond, each highly decorated with the attention we were becoming accustomed to. At the end of one alley a cedar door stood ajar. Although not overly ornate, its size, marginally larger than those of the surrounding houses, marked it out as significant. I peered in and called Philip over to see. From the door, tardis-like, stretched a vast hall as big as a courtyard. Exquisitely detailed tiling radiated from the centre of the floor and up the four-storey walls, to a point on the ceiling from which a glass chandelier hung, its elegant tentacles swooping almost half the distance back to the ground.

'That is the most sacred mosque of Morocco, forbidden to non-Muslims!' We drew back, wondering whether we'd caused offence. 'Look! Please look! It's only your feet that are forbidden, my friend.' Mohammed explained that this was the Kairaouine Mosque, the centre point of Islam in Morocco, governing timings of Ramadan and other important religious matters. The hall we were looking at was one of the smaller areas of prayer, in a site that often held up to 20,000 worshippers at a time (Anglican vicars could be forgiven one of the seven deadly sins considering this).

We hesitated before looking through a similar door a little further on, though Mohammed encouraged us in and past a sleeping guard with a machine gun on his lap, its worn paint suggesting long service. Philip and I stopped, but our man took me by the arm and led us on down a vaulted corridor. Before we'd reached the end of the dimly lit passageway a shouted command and the sound of boots on flagstone pulled us up once again.

'Quickly, come!' called Mohammed, gesturing that we should evade the approaching guard. In the time we'd been with him Mohammed seemed to have developed command of our senses and we inexplicably followed as he ducked behind a pillar and fled down another corridor. A glance at the intricate stonework about us gave me some confidence that we might not end our days in a hail of bullets just here; the guard would probably wait until we were out in the open, which, judging by the light up ahead, we were about to reach.

A hand sharply drew me back from behind. Philip also stopped, but Mohammed continued. Our guide had nearly made it to freedom when another barked order stopped him in his tracks. I hadn't a clue what was said, though I thought something like 'Stop or your accomplices die!' might be fair translation. Mohammed, somewhat brazenly when faced by an Uzi machine gun, started remonstrating with our captor, waving his arms about as one might at a traffic warden who has recently issued a ticket. In the midst of their heated exchange I asked whether we had violated a sacred space. 'Only if you worship money!' he said, looking pointedly to the guard. 'Do you have ten dirhams?' Less than a pound seemed little to secure our liberty, so it was duly handed over. The guard's countenance changed and, in one swift exchange, captor turned to host. He led us to the space Mohammed had been making for: an open-air courtyard surrounded by balconies of delicately carved wood. Along its length ran finely tiled fountains whose pools were sprinkled with rose petals. I asked whether this was ceremonial. Mohammed relayed the question to our host.

'No, team-building! Drinks reception for Renault Cars,' he said. I thought back to my days as a salesman in the wine

137

import trade and the pampering we occasionally received in the name of team harmony, with a small sense of wistfulness. However, I thought that maybe we weren't so badly off here with Mohammed. This was an opinion I'd soon be re-assessing.

Mohammed encouraged us to explore the courtyard and said we were free to take pictures. He disappeared for a few moments, though he could still be heard on a mobile phone behind a pillar. I wandered close and he snapped the handset shut and mouthed 'Mother' to me. 'Are you ready? You now come with me,' he continued, 'I have something special for you to see.' I fetched Philip and we were led out past our armed host and into the street once more.

The walkways became darker as we passed from the trade quarter, though they were none the less animated. Our pace was out of time with those darting about us: people who had long since lost fascination with their beguiling environment. Now away from the few tourists we had seen, and the money they might bring, poverty became more apparent. Plasterwork flaked from the walls and bits of masonry lay close to where they had fallen, swept aside only by passing feet. Dark holes provided passage for children. They appeared unaware of our presence as they played their games; some more aggressive than others – what appeared a harmless game of chase ending in a cornered child fighting his way out with a stick. Smells here were human and they brought with them a vivid sense of the medieval; the world of spice and perfume replaced by one less savoury. Our eyes found it hard to adjust to the gloom, and we followed Mohammed's silhouette, thankful that in his company we were being avoided by man and creature: some of the smaller and darker of which I tried not to identify. What trust had been built between us and our guide ebbed away as the paths narrowed and we began ducking beneath joists and avoiding coughing figures huddled against the walls.

'I wonder what Barbarella would make of this?' Philip mused, referring to our dominatrix sat-nav. From ahead, Mohammed asked who Barbarella was and we explained.

His cackle and wafting reply in the gloom seemed a little sinister to our ears.

'There's no satellite navigation for the medina. No, there'll never be for the medina ...'

A rancid stench had pervaded the atmosphere, stronger than that of the feral musk we were becoming used to. It seemed to be coming from the air above and even out of the walls themselves. It was a smell that had ingrained itself into everything about us over time. The little figure ahead stopped and waited, stooping by the entrance to a set of steps. 'Come, come, we are here.' Where was here? Was this the end game in Mohammed's protracted ensnarement? Philip seemed content to follow, so I did likewise. The narrow staircase took us three flights onto the roof of a building overlooking a dark square. Mohammed looked about us as if expecting something to happen. A door opened from a stairwell to one side and the shapes of three men approached. I looked to my friend without hint of blame; it seemed to me that we were now past that point. I wondered whether he was planning a few moves he'd picked up in the army and I weighed up the situation, as would an action hero, thinking how best to send the antagonists screaming into the night. A burst of light in the square below lit the scene like a flare, and I embarrassedly withdrew my arms from their kung fu stance and brushed a few flecks of dirt from my shoulder. The approaching men smiled as they saw Mohammed and greeted him heartily, quickly transferring their welcome to us. Philip and I walked to the edge of the roof and stared into the illuminated square below.

Beneath us a honeycomb of brightly coloured pits spread

from one side to the other, taking all available space. We were told that these were pools for natural dyes used to colour the goods we'd seen. Some of them indeed looked natural, the ochre possibly saffron and the blue indigo, but others seemed quite modern. We chose to believe them when we were told that the smell was a mixture of pigeon droppings and cow urine used in the process of tanning hides, as surely nothing man-made would intentionally replicate such a smell. Historically, human urine was used and the streets contained 'piss-pots' to allow passers by to contribute their effluent to the manufacturing process. Presumably this had to change when the medina became a world heritage site, though the conditions for those working in the dye pits would doubtless not have altered much. We were seeing their factory at its most beautiful, radiating its colours under artificial light in the cool of the evening; the scene might not be as beguiling for a worker at midday in 100-degree heat.

'Come in,' we were urged. This is it, I thought, the payoff: harden yourself against all buying urges and remain stony faced, you have enough carpets at home and Pam will look out of place in a pink jallaba at PTA meetings. I looked to Philip and could see he was of a similar mindset; we might get through this without buying some cheap fake likely produced in a sweatshop in Casablanca, if stories of such places are to be believed.

Mohammed and one of the other men led on, and the other two formed a rear guard as we negotiated a series of corridors and little rooms. The walls hung with shiny leather bags, diamante-studded belts and patchwork cushions that only Jimmy Hendrix might have looked cool on. We were asked if we liked anything. A firm but polite no was enough to send us through another maze, this time full of silks and garments. We again said no. Success! We had cleared stage two. At the next stage however, the level of the carpets, one of the players would reach 'game over'.

'That looks nice.' This was enough to trigger a complex and well-rehearsed scene, akin to the springing of a trap in an Indiana Jones movie. A table and tea set suddenly blocked our path (it might have materialised through the floor, such was the speed of its delivery) and a thin man in flowing robes with thinner lips and figure-of-eight spectacles emerged from behind a hanging rug, hovering like a cobra ready to strike.

With a click of his fingers the subject of Philip's utterance was thrown at his feet. 'You give me a price, any price, I shall not be offended.' Philip explained that he'd only indicated that it looked nice and didn't really need a carpet. 'Do you not like the carpet after all?' Philip said he didn't, the difference between liking and wanting too troublesome to convey. The man smiled and instructed one of his colleagues to take the offending article away, with a level of distain suggesting he wished the man to throw it from a window. 'We will find your carpet, my friend. We will show you only thirty carpets and make two piles, one for carpets that cause you insult and another for those that do not. There will be a carpet here to give you long life and eternal happiness. You have a wife?' Philip nodded. 'Your wife, she will beg of you to make love to her when you both pass on this carpet together.' Philip began to speak, but was cut short. 'I ask you not to speak, but to simply nod your head or to shake it as we pass with the carpets.' I'm not sure whether it was such mention of his wife, but Philip's resolve had been drawn from him. He looked to me, suggesting I might also like to take part. I averted my gaze; he was lost to me now. If we were climbers and he dangling helpless from a rope over a ledge, this was the stage to cut it; there was no saving him.

141

Each carpet was brought forward accompanied by sighs of appreciation from the group looking on, all except a tight-mouthed Englishman sipping his mint tea. Each came with guarantees of quality and promises of conjugal satisfaction, which if half true would surely lead to a sizeable population boom in the Cotswolds. I watched as the pile of rejected carpets was taken away and the selection process began once again with the pile Philip had shown appreciation of. The inevitable comment came after dividing the carpets a further three times: 'Congratulations, we have found your carpet! Now, you give me a price, whatever price you like, I shall not be offended.' Philip gave a suitably low price of around a hundred pounds. 'I am not offended!' said the man. All was not lost I thought, and I made to congratulate Philip. He reached for his wallet, but five leathery fingers were placed on his hand. 'But my price is eight thousand dirhams.' Six hundred pounds. The subsequent two and fro of barter continued for some minutes, Philip an un-seeded novice holding his own against the Federer of carpet sellers. As gripping as any final, the outcome was a draw 'on the face of it', I somewhat disparagingly said as we left (the men now dividing the money and switching off the lights behind us). But I was wrong. A visit to a local carpet seller after Philip's return indicated a fabulous bargain. The red and ochre rug with intricate pattern was indeed the genuine thing and Joanne was delighted with it when we got back – I only witnessed the delight on her face as he unrolled it of course, and can't say whether the guarantees that accompanied the purchase were genuine.

Mohammed led us to another riad (the term for these elegant dwellings receiving guests) for supper, and seemed contented to watch us eat from a distance instead of accepting our invitation to dine. As we walked back to our riad we offered him some money – which he graciously accepted without barter – and asked him whether guiding people was his profession. 'Yes, I like to help people,' he said, and beyond the furthest reaches of my cynicism, I think I believed him.

* * *

Three men leant against the old van with the sun behind them, their combined weight tilting the vehicle slightly. They were beyond the dusty péage at the end of the road from Fes to Meknes and we'd returned for the last of our inland appointments, before moving on to the coast for our final visit. My thoughts were firmly on this one however – the reason we had come to Morocco.

As Philip handed across the coins I strained to see whether we should have come in disguise. The silhouette standing to the rear of the van was lean and angular, sporting a baseball cap at a rakish angle. The second was shorter, too short to be Gérard, and hunched in a way you'd never expect to see our man, unless in a story featuring Notre Dame. The third, slightly fuller and striding over to where we were, showed promise; though unless M. Depardieu traded his golden locks for a tight mass of black curls when in Morocco, this was not him either. I had thought relief would be my reaction to his not being there, but I did feel a tinge of loss that we might not now be whisked into the world of a superstar and invited to feature in his next movie – about a man travelling to Morocco in search of the perfect wine. (Philip's filming was improving and I think he too had a few unaired hopes.) Of course he would have sent his entourage! There was still a chance – or threat.

Hamid, the man coming toward us, was another whom I quickly warmed to. He was laughing before we said anything, and we joined in, although it may have been our appearance that triggered the mirth. He called his two colleagues over, introducing them as Karim and Mahmoud. Karim was a good-looking man in his early thirties with a flowing walk, charming smile and thick eyebrows – one of which rose with an exaggerated air of suavity as he spoke. Mahmoud was his opposite. Although he had similar warmth in his eyes he was a shyer, smaller man, deferring to the other two. The three had me picturing the Marx brothers: Hamid was Chico, the in-between, Karim, was Groucho, and Mahmoud the diminutive Harpo. Hamid made the wine, Karim looked after the vines and Mahmoud, it seemed, just said little.

We were asked to follow their van. Even before we reached the vineyards things looked promising. We were again leaving the heat of the valley for the cooler hills. The sky had turned a deeper shade of blue, as if seen through tinted sunglasses, increasing the richness of the green vines and burnt orange of the vineyard soil when we arrived. At the estate entrance there was no sign indicating its purpose or ownership, in keeping with most others in Morocco. We had arrived at Les Deux Domaines, Gérard Depardieu's Moroccan venture.

We drove up to a cluster of sun-faded colonial buildings and stopped in a palm-shaded courtyard – more a dusty patch of earth where workers parked. A tractor shed abutted the whitewashed company offices, swallows darting about its rafters. The offices were clean and practical without the sheen of somewhere used to attracting visitors – delightfully un-Hollywood. I wondered whether to ask if Gérard was about, but thought it better to conduct the visit first.

Karim led us into the vineyards, which now yielded no surprise. The soils were as good as any we'd encountered on the trip and the care given to the vines indicated there was plenty of knowledge being applied to the project – the film star knew his stuff. I was told the vines were fifteen years old and just beginning to produce the type of grapes they wanted, which is why they'd only recently started making wine from them. This represents a considerable investment of time and money – try passing that business plan by a bank manager for a loan and see what they say!

Among the estate buildings sat a new one. Clean, white and functional, it was that of the winery; and a simpler example you couldn't hope to find. This was little more than what the French might call a 'garage' winery – the term applied to some of the smaller properties in Bordeaux that might invite derision should they call themselves 'Château'. 'We have room to expand,' Hamid explained, 'but we only make one wine here.'

There were two rooms to the winery. One contained the equipment to make the wine and the other the barrels to store it. Though small, the former felt spacious – uncluttered by the types of machinery required by those producing big volumes. Again, picking was done into small boxes, and grapes were rigorously sorted after being stripped of their stems. They were then crushed and transferred to vats by conveyor rather than pumps (the latter seen as too harsh on the juice). These were all processes only encountered at top estates. I began to wonder how M. Depardieu had amassed such knowledge of quality winemaking, and whether we were at the right estate at all, when I saw his signature on the doors of two wooden vats. I thought to casually point this out after the tasting. We were told that the juice was left in the vats to ferment at a low temperature in order to allow the more delicate flavours to be retained within the new wine.

The door to the barrel room was opened and a cool blast put goose bumps on my knees. On the air came the aromas of fresh oak – smells totally unlike the confected ones you find in some oaky wines. In many everyday brands the smell of oak is imparted by the addition of muslin bags containing oak chips to the vats. The comparison between the aromas conjured by these and those derived from ageing in barrel is similar to a comparison between tea bags made from factory floor sweepings and fresh leaf tea. Both types have their place of course, as they do with wine; I drink builders' tea out of preference, but I wouldn't bother writing tasting notes on it.

Hamid said that all of the wine was being aged in new oak barrels. Many use a mixture of new and older ones, he continued, but for them that would be a compromise, done only to save on costs – the new wood having the finest and most interesting aromatics to add to the wine's character. A peek into the Châteaux in Bordeaux will indicate only the pricier of them doing this.

As the property only made one wine, I expected the tasting wouldn't last long. Hamid gave me three glasses of wine directly from the casks and asked me what the difference was. I already knew that the grape was Syrah from the Graham Norton show, and I'd read enough Sherlock Holmes to tell me that the grape's name chalked onto the barrel might be a clue. I knew that they were all from the same vineyard and from the same year, the chalk again leaving my sensory skills untested. They were the same type of barrel too. I said surely the wines were the same, but Hamid smiled and encouraged me to taste.

I brought the first glass up to temperature with a cupped hand to help release the aromas. I began to second-guess the wine before smelling, thinking back to the time under the studio lights and remembering the aromas from then. Coming from a later year, how would this wine compare? Similarly to before, my nose plunged into an invisible cloud of aromatic particles with the joy of one entering a room full of their favourite pleasure. My nostrils channelled information in a rush to my brain, leaving room in my consciousness for little else. As the pen flowed, I was momentarily lost to the others. I then looked to what I had written for the first wine:

Intense and brooding, a monster of a wine, throwing out buckets of ripe black cherry and damask plum laced with vanilla pods and coffee beans, but still holding something in reserve. The taste is sensory heaven too: still a beast, but one who's been to finishing school. The structure is mouth stretching at this stage, the plentiful fine tannins accompanied by an elegant cleansing acidity and a mercurial viscosity, to give a feel on the palate that would shame many greater wines. Within this structure, like art in the Guggenheim, hangs an array of distinct aromatics, triggering the senses one after another. Firstly come fruits: ripe cherry, damson and almond; leading to a show of spices: cinnamon, nutmeg and black pepper; and onto one of barrel derived aromas: vanilla, ground coffee and dark chocolate.

It seemed the others had expected the tasting to be shorter too, as when I looked up only Hamid now remained. He got up from where he had been sitting patiently and explained that Philip had gone outside to do some filming, and the others had left to attend to an important matter. I tasted the other two wines a little more quickly. Whilst having similar aromas, they were structurally very different. The next was even richer than the first, but no better or worse for it. The last was the lightest, some might say understated, but again, no better or worse, simply different. The three wines put me in mind of the winery's team.

I gave a few speculative reasons for the difference, such as differing parts of the vineyard, but Hamid explained that they were in fact three separate vattings, and the difference was down to the way the yeasts had acted during fermentation. These three wines were a revelation, outstripping the one in the studio. But not only were they higher quality, they were simply too different to be the same wine.

'How come these are so different from your previous bottlings?' I asked.

'Oh, you've tasted our wine before? Let me show you.'

Hamid led me back to a room where Karim and Mahmoud's 'important matter' was on display. On a table sat a vast bowl of couscous topped with grilled courgette and carrot; next to it a steaming tajine of beef slow-cooked in Syrah and plums. At the centre of the table were four decanters. 'These three,' Hamid said, mixing small quantities from each into a glass for me 'are the Syrah wines you've just tasted.' The blend was harmonious, combining the structure of the three to produce a whole even greater than the sum of its parts. But it was still not the same wine as I'd tasted before. Hamid poured a cherry coloured wine from the fourth decanter into a new glass. 'Now taste this. It is from the Grenache vines we have. After you have tasted it, add a little to the blend in your other glass.' The wine was thick with candy flavours such as toffee and caramel, as well as those of boiling red fruit. It was sensory extravagance, an almost indecent display of aromatic exotica – Hollywood in a glass.

As I poured the Grenache into the Syrah, clouds of cherry orange billowed in the purple. I had to swirl the liquid for some time – the interloper taking time to assimilate. Once it had, the effect was alchemy, giving the potion a new dimension. The wine was now whole. Another actor had joined the Marx brothers in their performance and it was an Oscar-worthy one.

'Is M. Depardieu here?' I asked rather tentatively.

'We were surprised you hadn't asked before; it is the only conversation people desire of us sometimes,' replied Hamid. 'No, he is a busy man.'

Having noticed no helicopter or limousine I'd half expected this reply, but I was a little saddened. I felt that having tasted his wine again – and a further improved one at that – I could now say enough to make amends. (With hindsight, why I now wished to, having fulfilled my objective and visited the winery, I am not sure; obsession had probably begun to play its part.) I now thought to track him down when in Algeria. My research had indicated he had a vineyard there too, but I had no more than a line from a newspaper to go on.

'What do you know of M. Depardieu's project in Algeria?' I asked Hamid.

'I was not aware that he had one, but he has many interests we know nothing of,' he explained. I said that I would like to see the property when I was there and would he mind passing on my request. He said he'd try, but looked a little concerned.

'Are you going to Algeria? Not, I hope, by car!'

I explained that I would be flying there. I had arranged a visit with the state-owned producer for after my return in order to finish our North African quest. This seemed to reassure him little however.

'You will need to look more like me, my friend,' he laughed, and the trio, somewhat disconcertingly, made jokes about haircuts and suntans. I put what I had read on the Foreign Office website to the back of my mind and reassured myself that my Algerian contact had clearly said I 'would be taken care of.' I now saw the dual meaning of this phrase a little too clearly.

* * *

'Need some hashish?'

Not thinking that Morocco's laws were as liberal as to allow its sale in the supermarket we'd entered, I scanned the aisle for a banner headed 'Recreational Drugs.' Unsurprised by its absence, I looked back to the shop assistant kneeling by some pasta with his label gun. Maybe I had misunderstood him.

'Sorry?'

'Please do not be,' he said, 'I have large quantity – you like?'

'No, I don't smoke, thank you.'

He was undeterred. 'No, no, not for you, surely – for import, yes?' I decided not to enquire whether he had all of the correct licences and co-governmental agreements for his enterprise and asked him whether the store sold wine. He muttered something about it being bad for me and pointed out a shelf in the corner of the shop.

Having left our jolly trio with our stomachs full of beef and couscous, and our minds full of the knowledge that we'd found more great wine, we had driven through the afternoon to the coast north of Casablanca, close to where our final meeting would be the next morning. As a part of the filming schedule we had allocated the evening to do a cookery slot – thrusting our charismatic cameraman into the limelight so we could show our versatility to TV production companies. We'd sketched out a storyboard before we'd left, and over the weeks had honed it with creativity imparted by a glass or two of wine. We would combine the homely charm of Delia Smith, the cheeky nature of Jamie Oliver, the sophistication of Raymond Blanc, and give the piece a unique twist. Viewing the footage the following morning, we should have stuck to just the first three.

The first page of our storyboard now had a line through it. We had envisaged Philip wandering amongst stalls and haggling over fresh produce for his gastronomic masterpiece. However, a lack of markets on our three-hour journey from Meknes had led us to a convenience store on the coast. The store was only marginally more convenient than there not being one there at all and contained no fresh food, making things tricky for our chef. He seemed to find my suggestion of microwave burger and pan-fried cornflake in a ketchup jus unhelpful, so I had gone off to look at the wine selection.

The limited range was unremarkable, save for the fact that much of it could double as lighter fluid. For fun I bought a bottle that seemed to come with a warning: a picture of what looked like a dying camel in the Sahara – probably how you'd feel in the morning if you drank it. I'd pop it into a press blind tasting I was planning to hold back in the UK to show the scope of the country's output, and, mischievously, to see whether any journalist would wax lyrical about it! Philip looked questioningly as I returned with the plastic amphorae but he seemed satisfied with what he'd managed to find.

Earlier, as we were scouting for somewhere to buy food, fortune had smiled on us in the form of a sign with a tent on it. We returned and followed its direction to a pleasant looking eucalypt grove next to a cliff overlooking the sea. The campsite even had a permanently manned booth complete with ashtray; denoting it as the genuine article by our standards. Spotting a flickering computer behind the man in the booth, Philip asked if he had WiFi. I muffled a laugh, though my mirth stopped when he nodded and disappeared into a building behind the booth. He returned some moments later with a puzzled look on his face, as if we wished to interrogate the girl he had returned with: his daughter, Wifi.

I left Philip to explain and sought a spot to set up our impromptu kitchen.

There was no one else in the campsite except for an aged Australian couple who, judging by the sand build-up against their caravan tyres, were something of a permanent fixture. Probably not used to seeing others, they were instantly friendly in a way someone you have just dragged from quicksand might be. They watched with interest from a distance as we unpacked our cooking apparatus and set up behind the Land Rover.

Philip gave me a few pointers with the camera and I checked the light in a way I considered professional (from the perspective of an Australian onlooker, at least). There was light, and this I considered a good thing. In fact, to my untrained eye, the evening sun streaming through the trailing boughs of the gum tree behind Philip and his kitchen couldn't have provided a finer backdrop. The scene was set.

I opened a bottle of wine we'd bought from the supermarket in Fes and poured two glasses in order to toast the hope of getting something worthy on film. This is something that I now consider an unlikely occurrence at professional directorial debuts: the quality of output being more difficult to gauge when under the influence of a glass or so of fifteen per cent Carignan.

Instead of the intended mood-building snippets of Philip obtaining the ingredients, we decided to start the piece with him unpacking what he'd bought. After some footage of him removing spices from a Schwartz grinder with a hammer, and defrosting two anaemic sole on the warm bonnet, I put a line through this part of the storyboard too and set about clearing the branded packaging out of shot. I looked for a bin though there were none in the compound. There was one some way along the cliff, and, as I didn't think I was missing anything until the sole was up to temperature, I took a stroll towards it. A man on a scooter appeared and pointed to my bag of rubbish, indicating that I should give it to him, in exchange, of course, for a monetary reward. I was impressed by his entrepreneurial innovation so gave him a few coins and handed him the sack. He pocketed the coins, took the sack, and flung it over the cliff! He gave me a wave and drove off in the direction from which he'd come, genuinely pleased that he'd been able to help. Peering over the edge at the irretrievable bag revealed that I had not been his first client.

On my return I found the chef now up to speed with the fish and the work surface looking worthy of broadcast. The little fillets, lightly peppered with coloured spices, could have been coaxed from the seabed that morning instead of held in suspended animation for months at the bottom of a freezer. Our man had also found use for two of the three-dozen artichokes we'd been ripening in the back of the car for some days. In addition, he had pulverised some oven chips to create a 'bed of crushed potato' for the sole. I scanned the table through the viewfinder but it was out of focus. Adjusting the lens made no difference but I found that squinting did, and I was able to calibrate accordingly. I poured another couple of generous glasses out and sat behind the camera. I looked to stage three on the storyboard: Philip describing his ingredients and recipe, before the final frenzy of creation.

'You'll have to shout so the camera's microphone picks you up, your lapel mike's not working!' My directorial prowess had led me to the remedy, though we quickly realised the near-yell Philip needed to maintain to be picked up by the camera was doing little for ambiance. It seemed not to trouble our neighbours however, who had settled down to watch the entertainment on picnic chairs. They called over, asking whether we were famous. Flippantly, and somewhat influenced by the wine, I said our stage names were those of two famous chefs in the UK.

Not wishing to scratch another section from the storyboard, Philip suggested he tell me what was going to happen and I do a voiceover as he worked. Good idea, I thought at the time, though with hindsight this was too trusting of a man with an alcoholicly enhanced sense of the ridiculous. Had Philip been able to discern my commentary from where he was standing, he might have stopped me and given us some usable footage. In my defence, when he was viewing the dubious result the following morning, I pointed out that he was laughing. I however had to agree that the colour of the language, and the fact that within the short piece I'd managed to libel most celebrity chefs, might rule out a slot on mainstream television.

'That'll work.' I said confidently, switching off the camera to allow the water for the artichokes to come to the boil. 'How long will it take? We're losing the light.' I was now fully into my new role. Philip explained that the gas burners we had might be suitable for taking the chill out of cold hands, but were struggling with two litres of water.

The sun had dropped to the horizon and my thoughts turned to the bloodthirsty insects that were materialising about us. I wondered how long our repellent might hold out. We had applied enough to ward off everything including snakes, but we had found that there was always one mosquito within a swarm that had developed an uncanny taste for citrus. Whilst normally not a concern, an advice sheet printed from the NHS website had indicated that North Africa's only malaria hotspot was centred somewhere just outside the campsite. The advice had a consoling tone: 'If you are travelling within the area, there is no need for preventative measures in the form of anti-malarial drugs. The important thing,' it went on, was to 'prevent yourself from being bitten'. Whilst this might be consoling when viewed in Haslemere, it is not so whilst you are using the same rolled-up piece of paper to slap anything that feels remotely like one of the little bastards landing on your flesh. To our Australian audience it must have appeared that we had introduced a particularly violent form of Morris dancing to our filming schedule.

The water came to the boil and Philip began his final thrust of gastronomic creation. It was a tour de force, the fillets developing a crunchy spice coating in the virgin olive oil and fluffy potato melting a knob of fresh lemon butter. Sadly, due to the speedy nature of a Saharan sunset, this was not something witnessed by the camera. However as we were about to eat, I did find that inadvertently setting fire to the malaria fact sheet gave just enough light for Philip to briefly display the final product.

Having finished the delicious results, we poured another glass and considered whether we could have done any more to enhance the chances of Philip's rise to culinary stardom. Philip thought there were possibly a couple of minor points, though I said they were unlikely to affect his chances. Besides, he was already there in the eyes of two antipodeans as they bade us goodnight:

'See you in the morning Jamie, sleep well Raymond.'

* * *

The look of distain on the face of the man who'd asked us for money indicated an appreciation of music I'd not expected on handing him the Electric Love Anthems CD. Clearly an aficionado, he handed it back and walked off.

Having a few minutes to spare before our morning appointment, we'd stopped by the roadside to admire a river. Complete with water, it was an unusual phenomenon.

Morocco was in the grip of a drought and every sign we'd seen with a river's name on it simply announced a dusty path of strewn rocks. But here many took advantage: children swam, fishermen fished and others simply sat admiring the flow. It was a splash of life, both liquid and human, in the otherwise deserted valley. There was already warmth in the sun, but the aromas of the dew-moistened scrub were still fresh with morning cool.

We drove on to our meeting at Domaine des Ouled Thaleb, another Franco-Moroccan partnership we'd been told was producing some good wine. At the gate we pulled up behind a police car, whose driver was arguing with a bold security guard who seemed insistent on some point or other. The latter waved us in with a smile that quickly faded as he returned to the policeman. Two lines of well-established date palms, heavy with the growth of immature fruit, lined the entrance to a garden blossoming with colour. The sapphire blue of a swimming pool contrasted with the lush green of a freshly watered lawn. Elegant women in designer sunglasses sat on a shaded terrace in the company of men in bespoke tailoring, their sports car a key fob's click away in the lavender-lined car park. A waiter in a starched linen apron carrying a chilled glass of white lent the scene a colonial air – the boaters and flannels replaced by crisp Italian design.

We parked under a palm tree next to the winery, a 1920s-built stone building adjoining a terrace and a new atrium restaurant. A man in cowboy boots, jeans and white tee shirt was seated at the corner of the terrace with another in a suit who was taking notes. The first, a sturdy man with an even tan and European features, stood and beckoned us over. As we sat down, the other man left saying that, incidentally, the chief of police was waiting at the gate and was insistent on a meeting. Philip and I were taken aback at the response of the man in the boots.

'Tell him he'll have to wait: I have a meeting with these gentlemen.' This was Jacques, our host for the morning and winemaker for Thalvin, the French half of the partnership.

I asked him about Thalvin. He explained that the company had approached him when the estate was being regenerated twelve years earlier. He had only agreed to come as it was near to the sea. He said, 'Had it been Meknes, I would have stayed in Bordeaux.' When I asked whether this was to do with the potential for wine quality, he elaborated that he had to live near a beach and that his house, a few miles away, allowed him a morning swim.

The little oasis was the first coupling of a restaurant to a winery in Morocco, something else that one felt might have been more than partly organised with Jacques' personal comfort in mind. The menu was distinctly French, and the lush gardens, in stark contrast to the dry wilderness beyond, would be enough to convince anyone that an elongated spell away from home might not be too much to endure. It felt that the colonial era had not quite ended in this part of Morocco. Moreover, if this was a mini fiefdom, then it would surely be one encouraged by the accountants, as the estate's wines had topped most of the wine lists we'd seen. As well as quality, diversity was the key to success here – Jacques had been allowed the freedom to experiment and it was paying off.

At our tasting, comprising twenty-one different bottles, there seemed to be no corner of the market un-catered for. I asked what else he might possibly offer: a non-alcoholic wine for practising Muslims? He explained that others had tried this with little success (they must taste awful to those avoiding alcohol for religious reasons too), but he did make a wine with a lower level of alcohol. This, a fabulously scented Chenin Blanc, only six per cent, we drank later with lunch. Jacques explained that because in Morocco wine had to reach eleven per cent before legally being called wine, it remained unsold. I mischievously enquired whether he had considered bottling it with a guarantee: 'This is not Wine,' thereby gaining sizeable sales. He laughed, but did say he had another wine yet to be released; something he hoped would add a new rung to the quality ladder in Morocco. He then poured us a sample from barrel. It was Syrah from old vines, a style we had yet to taste in Africa. This time the enormity of the wine and the sheer abundance of aromatics made up for the fact that it was being tasted too young. It gave an explosion of flavour in the mouth that persisted long after we had left the tasting for a table set for lunch in the gardens. Although an unfinished wine, it was a definite contender for star of the trip.

Others joined us as we ate: friends and business acquaintances of Jacques, and more came and went asking questions, or to report on goings-on. The man in the suit returned and said the policeman was still at the gate. I think I overheard mention of a gift of wine to console the official that there'd be no meeting, though of course I could easily have been mistaken!

A gardener dead-heading rose bushes in the vineyard prompted Jacques to show us a picture on his mobile phone. Apparently the horticultural freedom allowed the man had gone to his head a few weeks previously. He had seeded marijuana plants amongst the vines in the hope of harvesting them before the pickers arrived. Part of his defence had been that they might prove a suitable alternative to roses in warning of fungal attack. He was asked to pull them up. I think it was another form of attack their presence would doubtless signal that concerned Jacques: blight by police helicopter.

Another character made himself known during the meal. Best described as an Arabian Norman Wisdom, his head appeared above the garden wall as he bounced on the other side trying to attract Jacques' attention. The security guard from the gate came to our table to ask what should be done. Our host indicated to let the man in and suggested he be given the task of cleaning what appeared to be an already immaculate van. The diminutive figure beamed as he was led to the vehicle, almost worshipful in his thanks. 'He has a problem with his mind,' Jacques explained. 'Everyone calls him "Le Petit Fou", but,' he continued, 'sometimes it's the mad ones that are the most interesting.'

At the other side of the garden a group of salesmen from a phone company (I didn't enquire which) from Casablanca were completing a celebratory lunch. They left the shade of their table for some entertainment the winery had provided. Donning sunglasses and mopping brows, they walked across to what looked to be the relative discomfort of a short rank of painted charabancs, each with a mule swishing at flies with its tail. To watch them leave the gardens and traverse a dusty plain into some distant woodland provided an enchanting scene, though when asked if we would like to follow, we declined. Our host said that the group were being taken to quite a spectacle and the journey would be a fun test for the Land Rover. It was suggested we let them reach their destination and follow later, behind a team from the winery carrying refreshments.

The rutted track indeed provided an assault course for our car (the contents of which were being churned about like balls in a lottery machine), but it appeared less of an ordeal than that experienced by the occupants of the newly polished van in front. Visible via its wildly swinging rear doors, the man responsible for cleaning it was still beaming as he clung on to a steaming tea urn: his pleasure possibly due to the fact that he might again be required to clean the van when he got back.

We pulled up at the edge of a ridge overlooking a mile-wide gorge. The setting was indeed worthy of wonder had one chanced upon it, but it might not warrant enduring the wrong end of a mule and its buzzing entourage for an hour to get to. The line of charabancs stood empty to one side so I asked where everyone had gone. Philippe (Jacques' number two, the man in the suit) pointed to the base of the valley. The group was just discernable gazing at an upstream stretch of the river we'd stopped by that morning. He smiled and raised his eyebrows. I did the same, to indicate I didn't understand. He laughed and said that being from England we were probably more used to a river with water in it; here it was a spectacle.

A stall was set up, which began to bow under an abundance of sweet pastries, the combined calorific value of which could provide a lifetime's energy for the lean waiter setting them out. Maybe not however for any of the clambering phone salesmen as they began to appear above the lip of the ridge; for some, a stall with respiratory equipment might have been more appropriate than baklava and tea.

Apart from a complaint that there was no mobile reception, the group made for pleasant company as afternoon slipped into early evening.

Having eaten more than our fill for that day, and with no pressing appointment the next morning, there seemed little reason to move on. The sight of the sun glinting on the meandering thread of water below had brought our fishing rods to mind too, so we asked Philippe if there was any reason we couldn't camp there. He looked concerned and said there could be an issue with our security, but said that he would call Jacques and ask. This he did, and said that we could stay, somewhat relieved that it was no longer his decision.

The silence after the group's departure was not something

160

we had noticed missing beforehand, but we now appreciated it as we sat with a glass of rosé and surveyed our domain for the evening. The valley channelled a light breeze up to meet us. The only other movement came from a mountain goat on the opposite slope and a plume of smoke some miles beyond. We took the car down a track and unpacked the fishing kit, content (having first checked) in the knowledge that we were not contravening any laws or under the scrutiny of cameras. This is not to say that we were not being watched.

The sight of the fishermen that morning gave us cause for belief that there might be something worth catching, but Philip and I lacked an important element that might assist our attempt: knowledge of what was being fished for. In fact, I lacked a second: ability, though this is something I rarely allow to trouble my occasional forays bank side. As long as there's a glass of wine close at hand, the rod becomes little more than an excuse to spend a day by a river contemplating life. If nothing's caught, there's always the chip shop.

Only a few moments after my first cast however, I detected a nibble on my Greenwell's Glory (as you might understand this was some relief – there was something worth fishing for). I cast the line once more and this time the little green and brown fly disappeared beneath the surface. The reel spun quickly, this was something big! I allowed the fish to run a little before striking, yet the hook leapt from the water when tugged, leaving me to cast again. This I did and the fly disappeared, but with the same eventual outcome. I tried once more, but instead of landing on the water, the hook slid down the back of the turtle that had emerged, no doubt wondering where these damned evasive flies were coming from. I decided that rather than risk investigation from the WWF (the nature people – the wrestlers probably wouldn't care) I ought to pack up.

As I reeled in the line I noticed a stirring in the bushes on the hillside above. Someone was watching us. I strained to see further movement though none came. While putting the fly back in its tin I used the reflective surface to scan the slope, continuing as if I'd noticed nothing whilst allowing my paranoia free rein. It seemed this time it was justified: a figure darted between two clumps of bushes, but remained hidden after I raised my sight. The braying of a donkey diverted me, but not for so long as to miss the figure boldly move further down behind some rocks, this time the shape of a rifle discernable in hand. Philip was fishing somewhere downstream – I had to warn him. I slid down into the river for the shelter of the bank and started to make my way to where I'd last seen him. Though shallow, the gentle flow covered thick sludge deposits, making progress slow. Where the bank dipped I was forced to crouch and push through the water out of the line of fire. I expected a face to appear at any moment above the reedy bank. The reeking carcass of a dead rodent floated by and its accompanying cloud of insects decided to give me their full attention. I got to the point where I had last seen Philip and parted the reeds on the bank. In front of me was a pair of brown feet in cracked leather sandals. By their side was the tip of a gnarled shepherd's stick. Next to that again was a pair of walking boots I'd become familiar with. I looked up to see Philip next to a shepherd boy, both viewing me questioningly.

Philip explained that he had called the boy over when he'd noticed him coming down the bank. Rather than wishing to think I was simply paranoid, I brushed myself down and considered that it was probably army training that had allowed my companion to tell friend from foe so comfortably. From the look on Philip's face, I saw he knew differently.

The boy however seemed worried and began trying to explain something in Arabic. He pointed to the hills and

162

tugged at Philip's arm. The donkey's braying came again, this time a little closer, hastening his efforts. He poked the end of his stick into the sand and tried to draw something, though with little success. (I still maintain it looked like a kangaroo.) He pointed again, this time to the setting sun and wagged his finger, which we took to mean we shouldn't be there after sundown. He started towards the car and motioned for us to follow him. The fervency of his efforts led us to concur that this might be for the best. He rode with us until the top of the ridge, where he jumped out to collect an old bicycle. We then followed him though some woodland. Although a little unnerved, we couldn't help but admire the atmosphere of Africa at dusk. The warm oaks lent the dry air a musky scent and the last of the evening sun cut through at a right angle, the trunks striking long shadows across our path. Once out of the woods, we slowly crossed a plain, the tyres of the cycle in front carving a thin trail in the red dust. I relished the calm of driving at the pace of a bicycle, and thought we should try it more often. We passed though a village of mud huts thronging with life. We slowed to hand out sweets to a group of children and were promptly mobbed. Our new friend began to shoo them away with a protective wave, though he relaxed when we indicated we were fine. Once the bag was empty, we joined in a game of football until the shepherd indicated it was time to go. Although we wondered where to, we were happy to trust him.

The track climbed through some pastureland sparsely dotted with sheep. The boy turned and proudly patted his chest, indicating it was his flock. The sun was setting beyond a thin sliver of sea on the horizon, its sparkle punctuated by the faint outline of Casablanca. We stopped at a corral where a number of paths met. Our charge, now happier that we had arrived, ran into a hut of painted wattle and daub. He

163

returned with a man. This time the shape of the instrument the man was carrying was unmistakable; the shotgun in the crook of his elbow was being loaded as he walked.

Had it not been in the arm of the guard we'd seen at the estate, it would have caused alarm. As it was, his smile convinced us that we were here for our protection. He simply said 'Jacques' and shook our hands, which we took to mean he had been asked to look out for us. He motioned for his son to light a fire and went back into the house. He reappeared with two tumblers of steaming tea before disappearing once more. This time he returned with a prepared chicken, which, once the fire was up to temperature, took centre stage in our evening meal along with some stone-cooked vegetables, the delicious creation of his wife who had briefly appeared at the door.

We now regretted having felt we could rely on French alone in the country, not appreciating that for a large proportion of the population it was a second language. I hoped our facial expressions conveyed our gratitude sufficiently.

The dancing orange light from the flames took over where the setting sun left off, giving the features of our host the texture of cracked leather. The sweet scent of smouldering wood mingled with those of the last morsels of chicken as they were devoured. The buzzing of a scooter intruded from out of the dark and the silhouette of a man wearing a pair of insect-spattered diving goggles presently pulled up, on his handlebars a Jack Russell dog. He was the first of many that evening who chose to interrupt their journey home with a visit to the fire. At one stage a group of eleven or more were gathered and we tentatively offered some wine. The man with the goggles accepted, much to the good-humoured taunting of his friends, but the rest were contented with another, more socially acceptable, drug – one grown even closer to home than the grapes for the wine, judging by some plants we'd seen. Laughter was the language of the evening and we somehow managed to exchange views without a common tongue. We even joined in with a boisterous song, the topic of which was Algeria. After it had finished I found myself still humming the chorus, which, due to the gesticulations that had accompanied it, I resolved not to repeat when I was there. I had been given the impression that Algeria's was a very formal society and criticism would not be viewed lightly by the state or its people. But even the most informative of guidebooks could not have adequately prepared me for what I would encounter.

The night had turned to early morning and the firewood to warm embers before we finally clambered a little unsteadily into our tent. The bush, earlier buzzing with nocturnal activity, was largely quiet, save for the occasional scuffling of some small mammal or other. At one stage a click was heard and I stuck my head out of the door-flap to see Kamal, the father, settling into one of our chairs for the night, the shotgun across his lap.

The smell of eggs frying on a stone and strong coffee awoke us, some time after when we had planned, and we gingerly descended the ladder and breakfasted with Kamal. As we munched on chunks of smoky home-made bread we showed him images from the trip on the back of our camera and did our best to explain our journey. When I said that we were leaving after breakfast to return to England, so I could fly out to Algeria, his thoughts needed no translation: he laughed and handed me the shotgun.

* * *

The three-day journey back through Spain and France was an uneventful procession of motorway services. We had no time for sightseeing, as I had yet to arrange a visa for Algeria and my visit was planned for two weeks' time.

The simple fresh food that we had encountered in Tunisia and Morocco had spoiled us, and, after our first anaemic vacuum-packed sandwiches, we decided only to eat when starvation beckoned.

We arrived back at Haslemere in the early hours of a misty Saturday morning and parted company. The last stage of the quest, due to visa restrictions and the conditions of my invitation, I would have to complete alone. Almost wistfully I watched as Philip ejected Barry from the CD slot and packed it away.

Out of Africa – England

It felt odd planning part of the adventure without Philip, though I reassured myself there would be nothing for him to do. I'd be flying in, meeting the country's only wine producer, and flying out again. It would be a short trip occupied largely by the tedium of air travel, and there would be little adventure; or so I thought.

* * *

It's a rainy summer morning a couple of days later in Kensington, and I have been in the same spot for two hours, in a queue outside the Algerian consulate. Presumably UK passport holders have taken the government's advice to avoid the country, as my features are at odds with the returning Algerians in line. I'm at the back of the queue and, as there's no advancement, I decide to eat my sandwich under some cover. I watch from a bus shelter as the line rapidly diminishes, but wait until everyone has left after they have handed in their visa applications. Gladly forgoing the rest of my Cornish grilled vegetable and couscous sandwich bought from a garage (eating anything from a garage without the distraction of having to keep a vehicle on the road makes it taste even worse), I make my way back across.

'We only accept visa applications between nine and twelve!'

167

I tell him that the door was closed until five to twelve and it is now only two minutes past. The clerk is unimpressed, and says I would have had my application accepted if I had been in the queue. I explain that I have come over sixty miles and ask if the tray next to him marked 'Visa Applications' might accommodate an extra one. He is affronted at my suggestion that he might contravene regulations and eyes me in a way that suggests security will be called if I persist. I stand my ground and look at him in a way I feel might crush his resolve, but it could have been my quivering lip that made him buckle.

'I have an option for you,' he said, leaning conspiratorially across. 'You can post it to me!'

'So you can open it and put it on that pile?'

'Yes,' he beamed, failing to observe the unsubtle irony. He looked to either side and slid across a folded piece of paper. It was a faded photocopy of a local map, with a post office circled in biro. A colleague walked past the office and the man motioned for me to take the map quickly. My resolve now diminished, I asked if there'd still be time for my application to go through if it reached him by post.

'Yes, and you can call me to check I've got it.'

'Will that be on the same number I have been trying to get through on for the last two weeks for details of application times?'

'Yes, I am a little busy.'

'I suppose that's the phone that has been ringing in the back office for the last few minutes?'

'Yes!' I left him still looking at me, working out how I'd guessed. As I walked to the post office, I wondered if there could be any other system that put the petty desires of bureaucracy before the needs of the individual in such a way.

'Cashier number one please.'

Having passed the five unmanned kiosks in my hour-long wait for postage, all perspective regarding Algerian officialdom was restored.

* * *

In a darkened room directly beneath the eaves I can feel the heat from the tiles radiating through the thin ceiling panels. The little window beyond the thickly lined curtain is open, but the air is still. I'm sitting by the head of a steel bedstead. A bead of sweat traces the line of my shin to the floor. I think to wipe it though the promise of more pain precludes movement. My back is bent and the nerves in my spine hint that should I try to make it to the loo they will punish me severely. I look to my passport and visa: taunting symbols of my foolishness, they are lying on a shelf just out of reach. I have been in much the same position for six hours now. The door swings open and a tray with food is brought in …

I take the tray as much for distraction as for nourishment. The smell of hot smoked salmon on rocket with balsamic vinegar and baby new potatoes fills the room. The glass of Californian Chardonnay next to it should prove a good match. The young girl carrying the tray explains that mum has gone to fetch the anti-inflammatory drugs for my back and should return shortly. She also lets me know that the charcoal I'd dropped by the car, when moving the sack to make way for my luggage, has been cleared up. The salmon turns to ashes in my mouth as I realise my visa runs out in a week and I have to get a new one.

'Good morning my friend, do you need another visa?'
　　'Yes indeed.' I say with a smile. I'm in good time and there's been no queue.

'I'm afraid I cannot accept applications on a Monday!'

'Cashier number one please.'

Into Africa – Algeria

I wash my hands and look at those doing the same in the ceiling-high mirror. They are sharp-suited, with new ties and highly buffed brogues. I am in worn trainers, faded jeans and a corduroy jacket with a rip on the pocket. I feel their pitying stares and their wonder that I can afford international air travel at all. I am at Heathrow's sparkling new Terminal 5 but little do they know I am dressed for purpose; a desire not to stand out in a country rife with poverty my aim.

On the flight I have time to contemplate passion, and what it is that makes a man ignore his government and travel to a country where, in some quarters, he will be viewed as a target. I console myself that my hosts have said I'll be looked after, and my usual grin when landing somewhere new still spreads as the plane touches down in Algiers. This is maintained as my fellow flyers and I filter through the arrivals gate, but fades when I fail to see anyone waiting for me. I lean against a pillar and wait as the throng disperses, confident that anyone sent for me should be able to pick out the only light skinned, long-haired male in the building. I try to call my contact, but the line is engaged. I've been told on no account to take a taxi. I wait until I am the only one left, and then make my way to the information point to enquire if anyone has been asking after me. Before I can stop her, the assistant presses the button on the tannoy and announces 'Mr Gimblett is here from England and looking for someone to pick him up'. Not what I had in mind. I suppress an embarrassed wave as all in the building look across. The only ones not to look are two men dressed in black suits and black shirts sitting at a nearby table. The larger of the two, a suave looking man with slicked back hair, folds his newspaper and rises whilst the other nonchalantly slides a coffee cup into the bin. They look about and make their way towards me. I see an armed guard at the exit and wonder whether I should seek help. The smaller of the two, a man with thin lips and darting eyes, assesses me as they approach, and I resist the desire to climb into the information booth with the assistant.

'Mr Gimblett?'

Noticing the handle of a gun beneath his belt, I respond in a pitch higher than I might have wished.

'Yes?'

'Welcome to Algiers. Was your flight early?'

I looked to my watch. I'd arrived half an hour early, having left twenty minutes late. The captain had said something about making up time and he'd obviously managed to. (I'd wondered at the time why they don't just get there as fast as they can anyhow.) Noticing that my grasp on the counter hadn't slackened, the men produced police ID badges and asked me to follow them. Speaking in Arabic into walkie-talkies (to one another as far as I could tell) they led me to a man dressed in a pinstripe suit standing by a highly polished saloon car. This was Jussef, my chauffeur. Either he didn't question why his bosses should wish him to convey a backpacker to their offices, or he hid it well. He guided me into the car and enquired into the comfort of my flight. Our undercover policemen followed in an unmarked sedan as I was whisked to the port of Algiers and the offices of my hosts, ONCV.

As we made our way into the city I pulled out an old picture of their offices that I had found on the web. In the faded image there was only one motorised vehicle along the half-mile stretch of gleaming white colonnade next to the port: a steam tractor loading giant wine barrels onto a cart bound for a clipper moored nearby. All other life, and there was plenty of it, was either man or horse-powered, and all were concerned with the commerce of shipping the country's wine to thirsty mouths far away. Three storeys high, and quarter of a mile long, the colonnade was home to hundreds of winery workers, and contained wine storage vats through which many millions of gallons pass a year: the produce of the world's largest exporter of wine.

As we pull up, I compare the picture, taken in the early 1900s, to the scene now before me. Next to us the sea is no longer visible for stacks of storage containers, above which only the tops of cranes protrude. The colonnade is now even busier, but the commerce suggested by welders, oil trucks and piles of electrical goods indicates that wine is no longer a major concern in this nook of the Mediterranean. Jussef waits patiently for a gap in traffic but our security overtakes and stops the flow to allow us into a car park. A shutter opens and he guides the car onto the ground floor of one of the arches, the headquarters of what I am told is Algeria's only wine producer. We park by a bank of vats that runs deep into the gloom. The aroma in the air is of stale petrol, rather than wine, so I look into a vat door.

'Those haven't been used in over twenty years,' Jussef informs me. The echoes of my tap on an empty barrel follow us up some stairs to the offices. They continue as his heels click on the polished marble floor, the corridor's frosted glass walls channelling the sound ahead, beyond thirty identical doors. Some are open, allowing a glimpse within; the sight of ashtrays, bronze reading lamps and the occasional typewriter evocative of an old detective movie. The end of the corridor is in darkness, abandoned. I am told that there are three similar corridors on this level and an identical floor above.

Jussef leads me to a reception office and fetches a strong coffee, almost a caricature of the one I had on the plane. He asks me to wait while he informs my hosts of my arrival. The room seems little used. A lifestyle magazine on a low glass table advertises clothing from a generation before, though it's the magazine and not the clothing that's dated. Pictures similar to the one I have in my pocket hang on the walls. I wonder if they were placed there originally, or as a reminder of the company's heyday.

Not for the first time I wondered why I was there. The country's reputation was all I needed to remind me that there would be a hundred office receptions leading to a better tasting experience than the one I was surely about to encounter. But it turned out I was already getting ahead of myself. I wouldn't be encountering any wine for seven days. From the itinerary I was now handed, I could see why my hosts had suggested a week-long visit (getting between vineyards involved air travel and day-long drives), but my only tasting was scheduled for the last day. As well as being frustrating for my research, the lack of wine was simply something alien to me. I thought I had somehow to remedy this.

Half an hour later, having been escorted to a heavily guarded hotel compound, I placed a tick by 'Day One: Arrive in Algiers and receive itinerary'. Having been advised not to leave the hotel, I contemplated how best to spend the afternoon other than sit in my room and dwell on the police presence outside. This was made somewhat easier by the fact that I had been installed not in an international chain, but a beautiful property dating from the colonial era, the best in

Algeria by the reckoning of its brochure. So instead I spent the afternoon sitting in my room wondering how my hosts had mistaken me for someone important.

'You are the first English writer I have seen,' said Anissa, as we climbed into the car to make our early flight to Oran. As she was the country's head winemaker, a position held for over ten years, this meant I was the first one since before the civil war. Wearing business dress and designer glasses she was not at all out of place in the Algiers I'd seen so far. She had been appointed as my guide for the week and, given her seniority, I began to feel a level of expectation that I wasn't sure I could live up to. I wondered if now was the time to explain that there'd surely been some mistake, but, as our men in black guided us past the formality of queuing at the check-in, I decided not to make a fuss.

On leaving Oran airport after landing, the familiarity of our new chauffeur's music cassette might otherwise have been heartening as we sped into the Atlas foothills; but it didn't feel much like '*another day in paradise*' as I was flung against the door every time we rounded a bend. The painted white rocks at the road's edge might well have briefly inconvenienced the progress of a bicycle into the abyss below, but for my taste they were entirely insufficient to discourage a car at times on two wheels itself. As I scrabbled behind the cushions for a seatbelt, Hassan, the chauffeur, leant back to me with a wink. 'It's OK, they are not required,' he said, having mistaken my fervent search as intent not to break the law in the presence of our new escort. With one police car in front and another behind, he was relishing the opportunity of driving at speeds mocking the limits. He also seemed keen to attach our car to the rear of the Panda in front, so I tried to brace myself and focus on the

175

stark beauty of this part of the Atlas range, rather than dwell on our likely imminent demise.

We were on our way to Mascara, a once legendary wine region in the mountains above Oran, but now considered a no-go area for most westerners. This was a landscape on the move. The foothills before the higher plateau were a series of vast friable mounds, barren of anything but the roots of dry grasses loosely holding the soil together. In parts the land had been gouged deeply by seasonal rains, and evidence of landslide was everywhere. One had been so recent as to leave a truck still teetering on the lip of the precipice. Now sitting on a rock, the driver had been able to crawl to safety, his expression dispassionate as we passed, apparently all too aware that our convoy would not be stopping. Cars quickly yielded on seeing the flashing lights in their rear view mirror, their deference placing them perilously close to the edge. Was I the only one to grasp the irony that wine was indirectly placing them in danger? I hoped there'd not be too high a price to pay for writing about it.

If I'd felt a little uncomfortable with this part of our journey, it was slight compared with my uneasiness when we reached the first signs of civilisation. I suspected the inhabitants of the former colonial outpost weren't appreciative of a police presence on their streets. They eyed the procession suspiciously as the horns parped warnings to all who crossed our path. I scanned my notes with a level of distraction that revealed I wasn't reading a word, but I found that when I did look and smile, it was reciprocated warmly. I told myself it must be authority that was at issue and people had no qualm with visitors. It was either that, or they thought I was a prisoner. As I'd only wanted to carry hand luggage I hadn't packed a razor, and the growth on my chin, along with my attire, made me appear as unlike someone who might warrant an escort as was possible. I wondered if the convoy would be attacked, and I freed.

This was one of many almost identical towns that I would pass through in the coming days. Laid out to a grid pattern, lined by trees with white painted trunks, they were created by the French in the 1800s to a blueprint. At their centre lay a Hotel de Ville with a courtyard and flowerbed, though these often showed the neglect of a country recently out of civil war. Here only bare earth remained where there had been blooms, and whilst cosmetic repairs had been made to the town hall, they'd clearly been carried out when there was no time or money for aesthetics. We passed an old boules pit. Its cracked mud and dry weeds suggested the game had long ceased to be something permitted by the luxury of leisure time. Acronyms and slogans were daubed on walls, some in support of the ruling party, the FLN (National Liberation Front), others less so. I asked a couple of questions, but since these were greeted by awkward responses, I decided to find out more.

The slogans dated from the recent conflict, which started with the country's first multi-party elections in 1991. In the first ballot the FLN, which had ruled since liberation in 1962, was trounced by the FIS (Islamic Salvation Front). The army wasn't too happy with the outcome and decided to cancel the second round, dissolve parliament, and re-install an FLN hardliner as president. As you can imagine, this sparked a bit of a fracas, which resulted in a decade of civil war and over 100,000 deaths. The conflict gave birth to a number of underground opposition groups, most of which had been defeated by, or accepted amnesty from, the government by 2002. One notably had not. Now having changed its name to Al-Qaeda (I wonder what's needed to permit the change – a franchise negotiation in a tent in

177

Pakistan?), the party formally known as GSPC vowed to continue its struggle, and has been responsible for kidnappings, car bombs and other attacks on foreign targets in order to make life uncomfortable for the government.

I was aware that this last fact was the reason for our cavalcade at the time, which grew as we headed out of the town and across the plateau. It seemed that our escort from Oran needed the protection of a more heavily armed local force. This, I hasten to add, is my conclusion at seeing two police off-road vehicles join in front and behind, and not something I was told – they could just have fancied a bit of a burn up, as the pace, somewhat inexplicably, increased.

Habitation became sparse and the roads less encumbered, thankfully making the going a little less exciting despite the speed. We had moved on a season since leaving Oran. Leaves on the trees were turning and the air held the dampness of recent rains. By the time I saw my first vines I regretted not having packed a jumper. The temperatures here were not dissimilar to the London I had left; this was not the climate I had expected.

It felt surreal traversing an otherwise quiet plain with no fewer than fifteen policemen. I wondered whether the sirens and lights were still necessary, as we were the only ones there to witness them – except, that is, for the military personnel in the vehicle that had pulled out to lead the way. I looked to the skies for air support and was disappointed to see only a buzzard. I now found it hard to suspend my disbelief at having travelled in such a way, for so long, to arrive at a vineyard where I would taste no wine.

Anissa pointed out some light green rows on the slopes in the distance (the Coteaux de Mascara, the best appellation in the country). She said this was a new Syrah vineyard – part of an ambitious modernisation programme where international varieties had been planted. She stressed that the

178

government had invested considerably countrywide since the days of strife – which at one stage had seen Al-Qaeda writing to the country's grape growers (from whom the ONCV buy) with a threat that if grapes were harvested for wine, they and their families would be killed.

Such dark thoughts, as well as my awareness of the armed entourage, were dispelled as we pulled up by a cream-coloured limestone wall, not dissimilar to one I'd leant across in Burgundy. Excitedly, I hopped from the car, vaulted the wall and used stones in the vineyard to pick my way through the damp brick-red earth to the vines. Anissa was alone in her delight for my enthusiasm: the police were seemingly unaware of the vineyard's potential as they hastily followed in their polished leather shoes. One of them had failed to observe a puddle beyond the wall and, as he slipped, there was some relief amongst his ducking colleagues that his machine gun's safety catch was on.

They stooped over me, curious, as I counted the neatly pruned arms on the trellised Syrah vine, notably at odds with the majority in the country. The rest were largely old Carignan and Cincault bush vines: a hangover from the French era. Not all hangovers are bad however (as I found in Tunisia with the Selian Carignan) and a little way off was a plot of thickly twisted monsters, sixty-year-old examples of the colonial variety. I asked whether the company had tried any individual bottlings using these or other vines like it, and was taken aback to learn that everything had always been blended for their Coteaux du Mascara label. Having not yet tried it, I decided to reserve judgement, but I knew I would somehow have to taste it before six days' time. As we made our way back to the car, I cursed my foolishness. We would, of course, be drinking it with lunch!

As the quarter of lamb was placed at the centre of our table, I sniffed at the glass I was presented and tried to discern an aromatic. Was it liquorice? No, that was too obvious. It was certainly a spice of sorts, though as we ate I struggled to place it. The guard sitting to my left explained that it was a secret recipe, and if I did identify the ingredients Algeria's answer to Coca-Cola it would make me a rich man.

Later that afternoon we arrived at a 'cave', one of the hundreds of sandstone buildings erected by the French for wine making. There had been many dotting the countryside throughout our trip, their red-tiled roofs like pins in a cushion of cereal crops where once had been vines. A small number of caves were still used by the ONCV. Others had been put to different uses, but the structure within them (two identical banks of square fermenting vats sitting atop those for storage) made them unsuitable for much, and most were crumbling shells from which little other than memories would now come. Anissa referred to these as 'ghosts', saying that her senior colleagues back in Algiers had worked in many of them.

'Please, Mr Gimblett, do not photograph that!'
Having tried to take a group photo earlier at lunch, I was now well aware that my security guards were camera shy (it was somehow hard to resist their request to delete it – they had also requested no video footage, though I did put my mobile phone's camera to use on occasion as a memento of my entourage), but I couldn't understand Anissa's reticence over the old wine press I was taking a snap of.

'We have much nicer presses now. That is something of our past,' she said, leading me inside. Admittedly the rusting post-war press would have done little for wine quality, though I forgave myself the mistake of thinking it was still in use, as, at first glance, the building seemed unchanged. The cave and vats inside dated from foundation in 1892, but, although empty of wine (bound for a bottling plant two days earlier), within the latter lurked subtle adaptations allowing ease of temperature control and cleaning: the two most important factors in good winemaking. Anissa pulled a tarpaulin from a shiny juice chiller, an Australian invention used to cool the pulp after the grapes are crushed: key for preserving aromas in a hot climate. These, along with the gleaming new press, were part of stage two in the modernisation programme that had started with the new vineyards. I was told the plans were still unfolding. As I viewed the open vat doors I wistfully wondered whether the changes had improved the wines: the few people in the trade I'd spoken to who'd tasted Algerian wine had viewed my quest with scepticism. As we descended once more to Oran, I was hopeful of something positive to report.

I ducked my head to avoid the stares of those in the petrol queue we were passing, suspecting they weren't exactly glad to see us. We swept to the front, forcing those at the pumps to either side. The queue had been over a mile long and there was a murmur of dissent. Here there were only men, and those with what might generously be described as faces with character; one or two bearing the scars of conflict. I had heard that the country's chief export was oil (at one stage outstripped by wine) and asked how it was possible that there were shortages.

'No, Mr Gimblett, those are smugglers, though they will not trouble us,' said one of the guards. It seemed the smugglers were keen to assist the country's export efforts in selling the contents of their tanks across the border in the less heavily subsidised economy of Morocco. I remarked that surely the border was closed.

'Yes, but only to those who do not know of ways.'

It fleetingly occurred to me that a crossing could have

been completed by Land Rover after all, but, as I jotted down a few descriptions of those about us, I decided the present travel arrangements were possibly more prudent.

As I made my way alone to a clandestine meeting that evening, after dining 'dry' with Anissa and a diminished retinue, I pondered whether I should call Phil Collins. If he wasn't receiving significant royalties from Algeria there was no justice in the world. I left him crooning to a sheik in the lift and made my way back to the restaurant.

We had booked into another impressive hotel on the outskirts of Oran. I had been delighted to see a mini bar in the room, though my excitement had been premature. Aside from a beer with an emaciated desert fox on the label, there was only a bottle of the cola I was coming close to overdosing on. I needed a glass of wine.

I made my way over to the Maitre d'Hotel with the short wine list I'd picked up at the door. He responded blankly when I asked if Gérard Depardieu had made any of the wines, so I asked if any of the six had not been produced by ONCV.

'No sir. They are the country's only good wine producer.'

'So there are others?'

'Yes, four or five, but they are not of export quality.'

'Why is that?'

'They do not have the expertise or resources of your hosts.'

The revelation that he knew who I was diminished my trust in his impartiality, so I decided to find out for myself.

'Are they easy to find?'

'To find them would be misfortune sir, but I believe there are wine shops in Algiers.'

I selected a wine; the best on the list, the equivalent of a pound more expensive than the others. This was to be the first six pounds of twelve I would spend during the course of the whole trip. (Periodically, and a little nervously, I struggled to imagine what my hosts were spending on me.) The Maitre d' said the wine would be sent to my room.

The bottle arrived a little warm, with a sticky red streak across the label. The cork was also raised above the lip – a sure sign that the wine had been exposed to excessive heat and expanded. I asked the room service waiter if they had any at a cooler temperature.

'No sir, they are all at the temperature of the room.'

'Would that room happen to be the kitchen?'

'Indeed, sir.'

I also noticed the year on the label. There are some wines that benefit from ageing, but I suspected that this would not be one of them. I asked him if 1993 was the current year and was told that for the hotel, it was. When he asked me if I knew how to use the corkscrew, my suspicions were confirmed: wine sales clearly did not form a major part of the hotel's revenue. Still, I opened the bottle and tasted the wine.

A little while later I sat in contented silence and placed my glass before me. I had found the aromatic I had been searching for: it was definitely aniseed. Having tried the wine and found it well past its best, I mixed in some cola to try and improve it (a practice popular in the Far East), but as this just served to ruin a perfectly good soft drink, I had stuck with the cola. I did try the beer, but quickly concluded that the fox must have played some part in its production.

* * *

The police car in front could barely be seen through the water cascading down the windscreen, the torrent giving the flashing lights and bright stripes an impressionistic feel. I wanted to ask Hassan if the wipers worked, but after the look he gave me when he caught me with the seats up searching for a seatbelt, I considered it best not to. He'd clearly learnt to drive in Tunisia and I was ignorant of such advanced techniques.

The sea the following morning, as we batted along the coast to Mostaganem, was as agitated as the heavens, the white peaks on the churning water the only thing distinguishing it from the leaden sky. Lightning struck the flaming towers in the oil fields, and where there were none it made do with lower objects, at one stage hitting the upturned crescent on a mosque roof. Having never attached religious symbolism to weather patterns, I didn't dwell on any connotation. Initially I had felt relatively exposed, now with only two police cars as escort, though consoled myself that the seaboard possibly offered less of a threat than the mountains. We were on our way to visit another new vineyard along the coast, and I'd been told it was something of a novelty.

Although not wishing to touch on my tasting experience the evening before, I casually broached the subject of wines from other companies with Anissa, and was given a similar line to that of the Maitre d': simply that the private producers were making inferior wine. Again, unsure whether this was the official line, I asked if we could visit a wine shop when back in Algiers. I said I would like to see something of the marketplace. I was surprised by the readily compliant response, though feared something had been lost in translation.

As we passed through each administrative department, we bade farewell to our police escort and were introduced to another for the next leg of our journey, a process involving a generous measure of hand shaking, backslapping and the occasional hug. After our third hand-over I stopped jotting down the names of our new wingmen,

184

as I was in danger of running out of paper by day's end. Morning slipped into afternoon as the car pressed on, somehow maintaining grip on the wet road. Anissa said the rains were much welcomed after a period of drought. I felt ungrateful in wishing them to stop but still eyed her seatbelt in front with envy.

After travelling a distance that would look substantial even when traced onto a map of the whole of Algeria (a country larger than Western Europe), we turned off the road and into some grassy mounds. We pulled up next to a wine cave with 'Clos St Jacques' carved above the doorway, but, as the archway and crumbling walls were all that remained, I didn't anticipate encountering any wine.

'These are Chardonnay vines!' Anissa looked expectant. Even Hassan, a non-drinker, seemed impressed. We had been content to travel in silence for a while and it took some moments for me to find my voice.

'They're lovely.'

As this seemed not to be sufficient analysis under the circumstances, I walked over to a vine and made some notes. I pondered whether it was the fact that we had travelled so far that had sapped my usual inquisitiveness. I told myself to snap out of it. I'd requested to see their country, and they were showing it to me. The best sites would inevitably not be conveniently located next to one another. The reason I had been brought to this vineyard is because Chardonnay is unusual in Algeria in that it produces white wine, a tiny percentage of the country's output. The company felt they now had the technology to make a good example. I noted that they were nice healthy plants; the sandy soil looked suitable and the coastal climate should prove beneficial for the grape. I supposed the reason I was less animated than normal was that visiting a vineyard without tasting the wine is like going to a theatre without seeing a performance.

185

Alternatively, it could have just been the first stages of cold turkey.

One way to tell you are in an oil-rich country is when petrol is used to barbeque prawns. Although the fuel's aroma concerned no one else when the smoking pile was brought to the table at lunch, I moved the ashtray lest a spark should create an inferno. I tried a prawn, though concerned for my taste buds I stuck with the grilled fish.

We were now at a seafront bistro a little way along the coast from the vineyard. I noticed a copy of my itinerary in one of the guard's hands. I asked about it and learnt that all of them had one. I was indignant, not at the fact that so far upwards of forty men with guns knew my exact whereabouts, but that their version ran to three pages. They were more informed than me! I was surprised to see that after lunch we were continuing some way on, to see another vineyard similar to the first. As we left, I did my best to cast any ungracious thoughts from my mind and instead focused on preparing some questions for when we arrived. I was glad to have done so.

The rain abated and the sun broke through. Impromptu rivers had formed carrying away mud that billowed red clouds into the sea where the flow met the surf. The copper green domes of small hilltop mosques shone as beacons for shepherds looking to pray. Storks harvested subterranean life exposed by cracks in the soil and muddy puddles filled the imperfections of a road becoming quieter as we drove on. Roaming goats and sheep now provided as great a hazard as potholes, forcing the convoy to thread its way more carefully.

When we eventually arrived at the vineyard I was impressed. Although potato and tomato plants had been barely visible above the waterlogged fields, the vine roots

186

did not have to suffer the same fate, as they had been planted on the best-drained soils. One reason for bad wine is poor drainage; it leads to fat boring grapes, which in turn give dull wine. Vines in the best vineyards often have to dig deep for their water, leading to more diverse aromatics with each layer of earth their roots pass through. Though these vines were too young yet for greatness, there was enough evidence here that they might already be yielding something quaffable; but I knew I would have to wait a while longer before finding out.

I was introduced to a small crowd who'd been waiting under a tarpaulin for our arrival. Now more comfortable with my VIP role, I somewhat regally passed down the line asking, 'How nice to meet you. So what do you do?' I was a little disappointed that no one bowed, but made allowance for cultural differences. I was surprised to find that the last person in line was a seaman, as his attire seemed far too smart. I asked him if he fished for prawns and explained that they were murdering them in local restaurants. Anissa quietly pointed out that I had not understood.

'Non, il est "Monsieur Le Maire," pas "Monsieur de la Mer".'

The man graciously said he would try to use his influence to have all seafood grilled in future.

After having spent some time amongst the vines we returned to the hotel in Oran, the necessity of having to remember names of guards I'd earlier met averted by my sleeping for the entire journey. This was perhaps the reason I was rather more alert that evening before dinner, my bonhomie abetted by downing two beers without concern for flavour.

Mustapha, the company's area manager, had joined Anissa and me at the hotel for dinner. Warm-faced and with wisdom hinted at by an enquiring eye, he was one of the company's old guard. He was smartly dressed in a dark suit. His hair was neatly parted and a well-trimmed moustache showed a pride in his appearance that outranked my own. Not that he paid it any heed as we stood in the reception. He asked if we should go through to dinner. It was my knowledge of the hotel's wine stock that prompted my suggestion.

'Let's go into town for dinner!'

Anissa said we didn't have security arranged but I said not to worry. Mustapha too seemed unconcerned, so we took his car into the city. Oran, he explained, was the country's party town, whereas Algiers was too formal, always putting money before pleasure. He said this was where people came to let their hair down. He assured me that folk here were cosmopolitan and tolerant, so I should have no need to worry. I needed no assurance, I was enjoying the buzzing walkways, animated street vendors and colourful shop fronts, but most of all, the sight of a bar advertising that it sold wine.

Anissa seemed concerned upon entering the bar, though I wasn't sure why as there were a number of other women there, and they were drinking. Until now I'd considered the reason she had not ordered wine was that we might have caused offence. I asked if she drank socially and she explained generally only with friends at home, and not in bars. I asked if she minded being there and she said of course not, although she would stick to orange juice.

'The Cintra' had been going strong for over a hundred years and could not have changed much. A two-storey saloon with a gallery and wall-sized mirror behind the bar, it had a frontier atmosphere. A band singing lively Berber music finally had me appreciating what could be done with a lute, though my enthusiasm would have to go some way to match that of some whirling businessmen, whose drunken efforts were wildly appreciated by their seated colleagues. Barmen, trays held high, glided between tightly packed tables, and heavily scented smoke hung in the air.

We ordered some steaks and frites. Mustapha offered me the wine list and asked what I would like to drink. Anissa glanced at him. Unsurprisingly, there were only the company's wines there, but there'd be no issue with old stock, judging by the laden tables about us. The list was also larger and boasted all the company's wines, including their best. Only a little more expensive than the rest, I felt it was not inappropriate to request it. Anissa seemed a little distracted but remained quiet. I put this down to the level of noise, which soon made the effort of conversing too great, so we waited for our order without speaking.

The wine I had ordered was called 'Cuvée du Président'. It was one I had heard of but not tasted. In truth, what I'd heard had been the reason for not trying it before. But that was back in the nineties, and a lot had changed since, judging by what I'd seen. As we waited I shouted to Mustapha, saying that the wine's name was surely a slur on the country's leader who, as a devout Muslim, didn't drink. Might not more hard-line Islamic elements view the president more favourably if he wasn't promoting alcohol? He laughed, saying that it was interesting I should see it that way, since the president in question was in fact the head of ONCV. When I said that surely the ONCV no longer had a president, but a Directeur Général, he eyed me thoughtfully and made a note on his pad.

'I will have words.'

He may have been humouring me, but from this point on my importance seemed inflated in his eyes.

The sommelier had no trouble with the bottle. With a flourish of a well-worn corkscrew it was open. He looked to Mustapha to ask whether he would like to taste it and the honour was passed to me. I said surely it was for Anissa to try, as she had made it. She shook her head and encouraged me to. A swirl and a sniff was all that was needed to say the wine was corked, the musty compost aroma unmistakable. I passed the glass on to my hosts to confirm my thoughts and the bottle was duly returned. 'Thank goodness' I thought, if the wine were meant to smell like that then I would be in trouble – all my aspirations for the country dashed in one sniff.

The next sample was poured. As the dark liquid splashed into the bottom of the glass I thought back to the moments in Tunisia and Morocco where my expectations had been exceeded. Would they be here? This was the cream of the country's production, a blend of old vine Carignan and Syrah amongst others. I imagined an elixir and a smile crossed my face. My hosts leaned in a little closer. I pulled out a notepad and readied my pen, then lifted the glass to my nose and wrote, 'Oh dear.'

Being written in my usual scrawl, the words were fortunately indiscernible, and I continued jotting some gobbledygook containing the word 'Help!' several times. The wine lacked flavour and had a dirty finish, indicating poor winemaking. I omitted a score in case it should be seen. I maintained my smile, which produced what appeared to be relief from Anissa. She gently pulled my glass from me, sniffed and smiled back, maybe just a little questioningly.

* * *

A deepening sense of foreboding accompanied my progress amongst the vineyards and in the many identical caves we visited during the following days, a sentiment I hoped I hid sufficiently in the face of mounting expectation. I was beginning to consider taking my chances by escaping my guards and fleeing the country rather than attend the tasting and debriefing session at the end of the week. I got to taste no more wine, but what bottles I saw did not give me hope. Storage was an issue, and the wine I had sampled topped every wine list; it seemed there was nothing better. I thought that maybe one of the private producers would provide proof that Algeria could produce top-flight wine, though that didn't really help. I was being treated like royalty, and so far I could only reciprocate by writing 'Oh dear'. I now feared my safety was in greater peril from my hosts, if I documented my thoughts truthfully at the tasting, rather than from Islamic extremists. However, I had a day's sightseeing scheduled before I had to worry about such matters. I could relax for a day.

* * *

My penultimate morning left me breathless and relieved that I was not there to chart the rise and fall of the many empires that had at one time ruled Oran. By lunchtime Anissa, Mustapha and I (plus guards) had visited: Phoenician sites, Roman remains, Spanish castles, a Turkish palace and a mosque. This was only the first leg of the sightseeing programme and I felt the burden of the diplomat greatly, but stoically held my own, apart from a couple of lapses that I hope didn't sour Anglo-Algerian relations.

'Mr Gimblett, this is the private toilet of the Bey, the Turkish governor of Oran.'

'Please give him my apologies, I hope he won't be offended.'

'He will not be, he died in the eighteenth century.'

I thought a rope cordon for the exhibit could help save further confusion, though didn't want to mention it.

Still undergoing restoration before opening to the public, the Bey's Palace and gardens had been expressly opened for me to view the government's efforts to encourage tourism. I can indeed add my endorsement by saying on the record that the rambling hillside residence will be a must-see when open. The pillared courtyards and stepped gardens overlooking the bay of Oran will be a delight to visit and the carefully cleaned wall paintings and tapestries should give pleasure even to those without the faintest interest in history. It might possibly be even more relaxing when the political situation improves and you don't need men with guns to show you round.

Also worth a visit is the nearby Pasha's Mosque, though you may not now be given access to all areas, due in part, I fear, to my visit. Connected to the Bey's Palace by a secret underground tunnel, it has a stunning minaret and half a dozen silver domes. The latter can be seen from the upper floors of some of the surrounding buildings and are very impressive. Clad in a shimmering metal, the tarnish of a little weathering only adds to their charm.

'What a wonderful roof!'

If the Imam does produce a twenty-foot ladder so that you and your entourage can view it from closer to, it is important you continue to be impressed. Standing amongst the domes the spiritual leader told me with some delight that the mosque had been granted money by the American government for cleaning the roof. I could understand his pleasure.

'And when will cleaning commence?'

'The programme was finished last month!'

I no longer wanted wine; I felt tranquillisers might be more appropriate: anything to stop me opening my mouth as much as to calm my spinning head. I spied a guard's schedule.

There was only one more historic site to go before visiting a beach. Despite wondering why I should be taken to one in late autumn, it was something that might prove less taxing on my failing command of French.

We arrived at the Santa Cruz Cathedral, perched on another outcrop above the city, and our guide, a soldier in loose-fitting uniform, let us in and began explaining its history. I watched mesmerised. He occasionally pushed the butt of his pistol to one side as his swinging arm caught it, his dark grainy face equally animated as he spoke. His was a well-rehearsed performance, Shakespearian in its caricature, eyes darting and lips moving between fearsome grimace and toothless smile. His Berber French was too thick and too fast for me to keep up with for more than a minute, so for half an hour I mimicked the expressions of surprise, joy and horror shown by my hosts and the guards, who were enthralled. I only once failed to portray the correct emotion.

'I am interested that you found the plague funny, Mr Gimblett,' said Mustapha as we left the building. His eyes twinkled. Thankfully he had noticed the slight delay in my responses and realised I hadn't understood a word. We drove on. I felt I could now relax and opened my window. The pine and undergrowth on the descent were redolent of Provence and I wanted the smell to accompany us. The window was promptly wound up. Thinking it was a mistake I unwound it, though my elbow rose once again with the glass. I smiled sheepishly at Hassan as he turned, realising it was for my protection.

We passed periodic checkpoints flanked with gun emplacements protected by sandbags. Here the police wore flak jackets. There seemed noticeably more military personnel on the road than civilians. My craving for a snooze was too strong to let this stop me, and I began to doze off. However, Mustapha soon thwarted my ambitions.

Uncharacteristically serious, he had chosen his moment to get something off his chest, and had waited until the Englishman's brain was beyond the ability for debate: a tactic possibly suggested by their secret service for diplomatic negotiations. Forget water torture or toe-clamps, if you need to grill someone, take them power sightseeing.

'As a boy, I used to visit that hill.'

Realising he was referring to Santa Cruz, I suggested that it was a lovely view.

'Do you know who I once saw?'

I thought of some sort of spiritual speculation, but decided against it.

'I saw your queen!'

Not knowing whether she had slighted him, I remained silent.

'Do you know why she was here?'

'For the wine?'

'To open up trade between our countries!'

I suspected she hadn't bought much, and tutted.

'Yes, since that day, the Germans, the Russians and the Italians have done much business with us ...'

I could see a pattern emerging, though he hadn't finished.

'Also the French of course, and even the Americans, especially the Americans! But nothing from you! Why?'

Mustapha leant back and Hassan turned and raised his eyebrows, though thankfully Anissa nudged him as a dog was crossing the road.

'We gave her a twenty-two-gun salute – even Chirac did not get that!' continued Mustapha.

'Especially Chirac!' Hassan added.

I was out of my depth and wondered how to formulate an official apology on behalf of our monarch without starting something serious. After all, it only took the death of an archduke to start the First World War.

'I'll do my best!' I said, making a note. I thought that this was ambiguous enough to imply I might give the old girl a ring without actually committing to it. Mustapha settled back, seemingly content. I was relieved. Thank God I wasn't being given a twenty-two-gun salute.

I suddenly felt sick. Having woken from the shallow sleep I had drifted into, I pulled my cheek from the car window and tried to discern where the noise had come from. It came again. The boom was louder this time, closer. A puff of smoke still hung in the air on the hillside, its form drifting out to sea, unchanged since the explosion. Two more came, one after the other, and the water some way out erupted with spray.

We were under attack, or worse …? Oh bugger, I was being given a twenty-two-gun salute!

Mustapha soon coaxed me out of the footwell and explained that we were passing an artillery firing range. A while later we stopped at a beachside café in a sandy cove. Mustapha bought me an ice cream. Whether this was because he felt he'd gone a little far in his grilling, or it was the next chapter in the diplomatic negotiation handbook, I wasn't sure.

Having an hour to spare before making it to the return flight to Algiers, we took a walk along the beach. Our three figures flanked by security strolling by the surf must have looked an odd sight. Mustapha's long coat flapped in the wind coming off the sea and Anissa dug her hands into her pockets as we discussed their export ambitions with the UK. The implied expectation of me only served to cement my impending sense of doom as we said goodbye to Mustapha and left Oran, bound for the second leg of sightseeing in Algiers before The Tasting.

Having landed at Algiers airport we waited a few moments before clearing Customs. This was due to an intricate combination of stamps required, rather than security. Prior to boarding in Oran, a heavily robed man had passed through the metal detector before me and, as the alarm sounded, held aloft a mobile phone. He was waved on board without any further checks. Having been about to throw away my newly purchased razor and a corkscrew I decided to take my chances and leave them in the bag that I was about to put through the x-ray machine.

Leaving the airport in Algiers I was delighted to know that I would be freshly shaven for my tasting in the morning, but it did cross my mind that it still might be prudent to lose the corkscrew.

* * *

A line of dead bodies is always a grim sight, especially when you feel partly responsible.

As an Englishman, I haven't experienced the sense of collective guilt that must be felt by Germans, Japanese and other nations made aware of their actions after a conflict (whether we have simply been nicer than others, or as victors have been able to write the histories to suit us, is another matter). We were at a museum beneath the twenty-storey high Monument of Independence perched on a ridge above Algiers. Seeing the images of 'atrocities and genocide' committed by the French during the War of Independence in 1962, gave me insight into a side of the story not widely heard by northern Europeans. It made grim viewing. I consoled myself that my French grandfather had fought another foe, and in the Second World War, so it was the country of his birth rather than his generation that was responsible. Nonetheless, I chose to remain entirely English

196

in the eyes of the passionate military guide who led us around. After the museum, he took us into a private mausoleum to sign a book reserved for foreign dignitaries to commemorate the dead. I looked suitably sombre as he opened the weighty tome and handed me a pen. I hoped that my demeanour compensated for the fact that I would likely be the first to sign in trainers and a tee shirt. The pen didn't work and another was handed to me, but the ink in this one took some while to flow. The guide looked embarrassed, little realising that it was probably divine intervention.

There was just one visit left before my tasting the next morning. As I had orchestrated that myself, I knew what I was in for: a quick stop at an off-licence to see what the competition was up to and buy something that would prove the country capable of making great wine (I was even prepared to settle for 'drinkable' at this stage).

I was surprised to find that a trip to an off-licence in Algiers required a bolstering of security. An unmarked car joined our police retinue and four Special Forces officers got out. Although the welcome was warm and mutual, my police escort could not have felt anything but envy at the size of their guns. We drove a short way through the city to the walls of the kasbah – an odd spot for a shop selling alcohol, I thought. The Algerian equivalent of a medina, the kasbah is the Islamic heart of a city. This one was more utilitarian than anything we'd seen in Morocco or Tunisia though, where, in parts, tourism had touched the streets.

It was late afternoon and thronging. People traded all manner of fresh produce and manufactured goods from doorways, stalls and even their pockets. Much of what I saw was only glimpsed from between the shoulders of my guards or over the head of the shortest of them. The further we made our way into the kasbah the more we stuck out. Ahead the alley opened into a square where a crowd was gathered. My entourage stopped to listen. They stiffened a little. I assumed the man I could see on the steps at the far end of the square was not promoting soap powder. If he was, the crowd was very receptive and should be buying enough for him to retire on. The guards' walkie-talkies crackled to life and everyone talked into them at once. Although the language barrier again precluded me from discerning whether they were just speaking to one another, I suspected the shortest said something like 'Bugger!'

The crowd, now rather enthused, dispersed and filtered from the square. Although they were possibly all just keen to get to a supermarket, my guards were taking no chances. We ducked into an alley, which, for eight people with guns is not easily achieved. (Well, six with guns, as they had omitted bringing any for Anissa or me.) The shortest guard encouraged me to stop peering over his head (I think he had a Napoleon complex) and they huddled around me as the crowd streamed past. I was too overwhelmed by matters of personal hygiene to be overly concerned, but obediently kept my head as low as my nostrils permitted.

The crowd passed by and we made our way a little quicker. We presently came to a doorway with baskets of vegetables piled up on both sides, and went in. A set of narrow steps led to an underground warehouse bubbling with commerce. Heads turned and conversations stopped as we passed, as if it were unusual to be shopping in such a manner! The short guard held his machine gun across his chest in readiness should one of the goats try its luck. I spotted a fish stall where prawns spilled from a plastic tub and took a sniff: they were so fresh there was no hint of petrol. A man chopping at a side of lamb narrowly avoided adding his fingers to a customer's order when he saw the procession. His disapproving stare suggested I would have been held liable for any lost digit. Although this was not the same layout as Aldi, I expected the wine would be at the back and was happy to make my way through, all the while assiduously trying to avoid eye contact. If there was ever a time to give up alcohol and try a new career, it was now. The sight of soap powder in an oil drum meant we were in household goods (a lack of customers confirming my earlier suspicions). With no mineral water section, or party dips for that matter, I had hoped the wine would be next, but there was none, and I was swept up a set of stairs and out into another street.

'Did you enjoy the marketplace?'

Aha! My poor French of earlier had come home to roost. Vowing to brush up on my vocabulary, I asked Anissa if we could visit a shop selling wine and she showed me that it was next on the new itinerary, after the marketplace I had requested to see. With hindsight it was a part of Algiers I am delighted to have encountered, though one I may wait for a while before returning to.

Visiting a wine shop is normally a joy for me, but this was something special. Although the uncontained pleasure I displayed at viewing the wall of bottles was probably inappropriate, I didn't care. I handled each as a grail, examining them to determine my selection. The prime subject of my attention was the address at the bottom of each label. Those made by the ONCV, the ones I'd get to taste in the morning, I put back on the shelf, others I set to one side. Anissa seemed more than content just to watch me. After some minutes I had five bottles. There were four whose lack of quality was all too apparent without even opening them, the paleness of the glass allowing me to see the brown cloudy wine within. These I returned to the shelf. The last bottle would be the one I would pin my hopes on. Tapered like the trendiest of Chilean bottles, it had thick dark glass and a neat parchment label with a watercolour of the Santa

Cruz Cathedral. The vintage was recent too. Best of all it was from the Coteaux du Mascara and proclaimed to be from old vines. It suddenly occurred to me that if Gérard Depardieu were making a wine in Algeria this would be it. The price was also higher than that of any of the ONCV wines. I rummaged for the money but Anissa graciously went to buy it for me. Feeling that the final insult would be for my host to purchase another producer's wine for me (and probably the only bottle I would be reviewing positively), I insisted to the contrary. But before I could stop her, the cash was whisked from her hand. The cleft stick I had found myself trapped in pinched a little harder.

Now back in the hotel I'd vacated a week earlier, I listened from my balcony to Algiers at dusk. Haunting chants from the hills behind the ancient city drifted down and mingled with the whistles and horns of the jammed streets, which lay beyond the peace of the gardens below. I pressed the off button on the television to rid the air of a frenetic Arabic game show. The screen flickered to a red dot and the dark room was in silence. Before me on the balcony table sat my corkscrew, a glass and the bottle. I waited some time before opening it. I had been in the trade for twenty years and had never craved wine as I did now. I wanted to prove to myself that I had not become an alcoholic, and could resist temptation. I jotted down the address on the label and wondered if maybe it might lead me to the person I had sought the entire trip, but that was a discovery for another day.

The cork came easily, not too loose or firm. Clean and smooth, it was free of the dusty pockmarks of cheaper examples. I hadn't the luxury of a candle and preferred the atmosphere in the half-light, so raised the glass to the bottle lip and poured slowly, so as not to disturb any sediment. I considered the semi-regal treatment I had encountered in the last week and wondered whether I should just drink the stuff and not make any notes, but knew I had to. I gripped the stem, closed my eyes and lifted.

I felt my temples pinch, white lights danced before my eyes and my head flung back. I reached for my pen:

The nose is a painful cacophony of ammonia and excrement swirling with a fungal stench – a sensation similar to having an old soiled nappy thrust beneath your nose whilst being punched in both ears.

I flung the offending liquid into a flowerbed below and was surprised not to see the plants wilt. I switched the light on, something I should have done before. I hesitated before pouring another glass, though I had to see it.

I looked into the glass. Although nothing moved in the thin gruel, I assumed that it was because the liquid had long killed the matter floating on the surface. 'A violent shade of red billowing with tiny black specks,' was my note for the colour.

'For the book!' I thought. I had to taste it for the book. The bathroom would be the best place, making for quickest disposal after tasting. I went in with the glass and looked at myself in the mirror. I wondered whether it was worth it, I was quite good at carpentry and had trained as a chef ... No, it had to be done. I raised the liquid to my lips, though quickly placed it down and walked back to the balcony. Something within me was not allowing self-harm of this magnitude. I braced myself, ran back to the wine and without thinking took a slurp. I had the presence of mind to place the glass back on the cabinet rather than let it slip from my fingers and smash on the floor, though I couldn't help showering the mirror and light as I spat the liquid back out. It took some moments to compose myself enough to pen a note for the palate:

Best described as bloated and gangrenous, the body attacks the palate like a zombie with a hatchet. Even after ejection the liquid continues to crawl about the mouth seeking purchase, leaving you grappling with fetid horrors on the length.

In the morning I found that I had omitted to score the wine, though felt it might be best left unclassified. An evening's contemplation had led me to two conclusions: I could now say I probably wasn't an alcoholic, as I had resisted further temptation; and I could report to my hosts that their wine was indeed the best in the country. Both of these were small consolation as the police cleared the gridlocked streets so I could make the tasting on time. I wondered if winding the window down and taunting those we were passing might spare me the fate that awaited me.

We arrived at the tasting destination: a restaurant perched at the end of a jetty near to the colonnade I'd visited on the first day. It was a tranquil setting a little way out from the commerce of the dockside. I looked to the moored fishing boats as a possible escape route, but realised I must face the people who had been so nice to me and tell them I didn't like their wine. I would offer to cover the cost of the week even though I knew it would mean a letter to my mortgage lender. It was the noble thing to do, something that would make them proud to have met an Englishman. Then it occurred to me: I could lie!

The pillared building had a central atrium with a counter piled with crushed ice. It was before lunchtime and one of the staff was selecting produce from a fisherman with a heavy bucket. Pictures of Algeria's great and good lined the walls: past presidents and other notables. Flowers had been put out. Crisp linen and silverware had been laid on all but one table. On this stood a row of bottles, a sight that, up until the evening in Oran, I had longed for. Behind the bottles stood a crowd of people. Judging by their expectant faces they had been told that the scruffy man walking toward them was somehow important. One of the men looked vaguely familiar. I looked back to the paintings on the wall and noted a likeness.

'This is M. Madjid, the company's Directeur Général. He has cut short a meeting with the Minster of Agriculture to be here.'

Oh good. 'Delighted to meet you.'

Anissa introduced me to her colleagues, including winemakers and technicians specially summoned from other parts of the country to be there. My carbon footprint for the trip was not looking good. They were curious to hear my views and asked what I had thought of the vineyards I had seen. On easy ground, I was able to please without falsehood and said what marvellous sites they had, comparing the microclimates to those of Spain and the soils to some of the world's best. I was told that they had come because they wanted to hear my opinions on their wines. As Anissa opened the bottles, I decided that they might not wish to know, and thought of what to say instead. But it was too late. The first glass was upon me, as were the eyes of all around.

I quickly nosed and tasted, then jettisoned the liquid into a spittoon. The Directeur Général spoke before I could formulate a note.

'What do you think?'

'It's very nice!'

He smiled and looked back to the others, and they did so in turn, with a small amount of relief rather than sycophanti-cally. Their relief, however, could not have matched mine. I hadn't had to lie. I would be able to describe exactly what I thought of the wine without fear of being cast into the bay. The tasting continued in the same vein, each wine a little better than the last. I was becoming quite animated. Short of giving 'high-fives', I think I conveyed my feelings adequately. Lastly, we came to the bottle I had come across at the bar in Oran: Cuvée du Président, supposedly the best in the country. Having already tried it I knew it wasn't in the same league as any of those I'd just praised. At least I felt I could now say so with impunity, but decided to withhold judgement.

Anissa poured the wine and looked to me expectantly. I knew I had to disappoint. I tasted the wine and felt an immediate crisis of confidence. There was something wrong with my palate! This wine was good, nothing like the bottle in the bar. Was I drunk? I ruled this out as I had spat out every drop so far. Was the level of expectation from my hosts influencing me? No, I couldn't have imagined a greater difference had a gun been place to my head. The other bottle had been made from dirty, low quality grapes and had lacked body and aroma, but this was rich, supple and flavoursome. I looked to Anissa.

'You have noticed a difference with the one we had in Oran?'

When I confessed that I didn't think they were the same wine, she revealed that the bottles before me were of export quality, whereas the others I had encountered were for the internal market. This was the reason the company hadn't wanted me to taste any wine on our trip. I could have hugged her: I hadn't lost my ability to taste and moreover, I had found some good wines.

During the debriefing session back at the offices with Anissa and the Directeur Général that afternoon it was explained that economically it was simply not viable to produce the same quality of wine for the home market as for export, but they were trying to close the gap. It wasn't mentioned, but I suspected that the government preferred investments to be channelled into export efforts rather than risk being seen to promote drinking locally. I thought that any decision to convert to Islam and forego alcohol would be made that much easier in a country where there were wines like the one I had tasted the night before, which, I had concluded, could not have been Gérard Depardieu's.

I sat back becalmed in the leather chair and leafed through the glossy brochure charting the next stages of the modernisation programme. Amongst artists' impressions of new storage tanks and bottling installations was a photograph of two vats I had seen in Morocco, with Gérard's signature clearly visible on each door.

'You've visited M. Depardieu's property in Morocco?' I asked.

'No, no, those are his, but here in the mountains near Mascara,' explained Anissa.

I knew the actor was unflappable, but his bravery knew no bounds! His neighbours in Mascara would surely wish him worse than those in *Jean de Florette*, who merely wanted unscrupulously to buy his land. To my image of a wheelbarrow and secateurs, I added a bullet-proof vest. I wondered if the poor man knew that he had been subjected to industrial espionage from the ONCV. As if he didn't have enough to contend with! I thought I'd now do a little prying of my own in order to find out what else they knew, and assist my Gallic hero in his efforts.

After a few minutes of incisive questioning I found I was a natural interrogator. Without having to resort to instruments of torture, I managed to ascertain that they knew the age of his vines, how the wine was made, the quantity, and that it was only exported. They were singing like canaries. Shamelessly, Anissa even flaunted a bottle. It was

Depardieu's wine all right. His face beamed from the back label as it had done on his Moroccan bottle, and the text was similar too, describing how the vines were meticulously tended (without any mention of the danger faced). I wondered how I might get a taste; after all, this could be the only bottle in the country. Anissa, sensing my desire, unexpectedly offered to open it. I asked if she might, but surely wouldn't they need it for their own purposes?

'We have many more in storage.'

This was brazen. My man was up against an unrepentant adversary indeed. I tried not to show my anticipation as she pulled the cork, and remained impassionate as I tasted the wine, which, a powerful mouthful, was the best I'd encountered in Algeria. The country's potential was indeed being realised, but not by those with the greatest resources. It took an interloper, toiling under the most adverse conditions, to unlock from the soil what was always there. This begged a question.

'Have you tried making a similar wine?'

'But I made this wine,' Anissa responded.

'But, surely, Gérard ...'

'He visited the vineyards of course, in a similar manner to you. But it is a marketing partnership, as with many of his wines.'

My mind reeled.

'Not Morocco too?'

'Yes, I understand in Morocco also.'

This was too much. Whatever next? Father Christmas and the tooth fairy had been bad enough. I composed myself and finished the debrief, complimenting my hosts on the wine and saying I looked forward to seeing others they were thinking of making to a similar style. Maybe sensing my inner angst as we bade each other farewell, Anissa kindly gave me the bottle; a generous host to the end. This was welcome medicine to settle a mind spinning with thoughts of betrayal. Could I ever trust again?

Back on my balcony the experience was entirely unlike the evening before. Although the room was again unlit and the sounds and scents of the city were the same, the wine was now an orchestra playing a symphony of aromas that immersed my senses (instead of a thrash metal band clubbing me with a guitar), allowing me to drift through my memories of the past week.

My trips to the vineyards had reminded me of the time had I spent in Chile and Argentina in the early nineties. Then, the talk had been of potential (one that has now been realised). Here, as well as in Tunisia and Morocco, the talk had been the same. These African countries could produce wine to compete with the very best, and they now were beginning to do so; but the world had yet to cotton on, if indeed it ever would due to cultural barriers. In the meantime, I consoled myself that I was enjoying a wine that, if the world did take notice, would probably cost ten times as much. This thought, coupled with the fact that it was the first wine I had not spat out in a week, hastened the end of the bottle.

With only a glass remaining clarity of thought seemed sharper, which was, as is the way, the inverse of reality. And so it was that I decided to take a stroll. It may have been a desire to get away from a room where I had believed in something that was now cruelly dispelled, or perhaps that I wanted to be master of my own movements for the first time in a week, but it was more likely just the result of having drunk too much that found me hiding behind a date palm as a guard passed the rear doors of the hotel.

The grass beneath the tree was damp, the work of a sprinkler system I would have to avoid in reaching the outer wall. It was late enough for the balconies above to be in darkness and there was no moon. Two cameras scanned the grounds from the corners of the hotel. Every third sweep they made had them pointing in opposite directions, allowing me a blind spot. I held a hotel brochure in my hand, but crumpled it in disgust; the grounds were not to scale. A dog could be heard at the other side of the compound, but I knew it to be chained. My moment had come. I steadied the stoppered bottle in my jacket pocket and broke cover. A jet of water caught my ankle, but nothing more hindered my dash to the wall, a high stone-built barrier topped with razor wire. The guard returned from around the corner of the hotel. I crouched in the shadows, waiting for him to pass, and took another swig from the bottle. The wine had lost none of its intensity and gave me the boost I needed for the next stage. I would have to pass the sentries at a gate a little way along the wall, one of two barriers to be breached if I was to reach freedom. I made my way as close as I dared, then waited, and watched.

A laundry van pulled up and the barrier opened, allowing me to slip past undetected. This was easy, but I knew the next was more heavily guarded. Beyond the outer gardens lay the final perimeter. There were stinger traps and four armed officers between me and Algiers. I watched from a bush as a car pulled in and was searched with mirrors. This was going to be tricky. Three women in hijab, obscured but for their eyes, left the compound. This gave me an idea, but one I quickly dismissed as, thankfully, I wasn't that drunk. There was only one thing for it: bribery. I'd use my unspent dinars to secure my passage.

Tucking the bottle out of sight, I emerged from the bush, without thought for an explanation as to why I was there in the first place. I strode nonchalantly toward the guards. They seemed unconcerned. This was good; the wine hadn't affected my gait. I hesitated before rummaging in my pocket for the notes lest I arouse suspicion that I was reaching for a concealed weapon. I approached the first two guards but, as they stayed at their posts, I coolly continued past, stepping over the spikes stretched across the road. As I neared the outer barrier one of the final pair of sentries shuffled his machine-gun further onto his back and eyed me. This was the time to produce the cash, I thought, and made for my pocket. But before I could do so, he opened the barrier and ushered me through.

'Aren't you going to stop me?' I questioned.

'No, of course not.'

Freedom!

'My job is to stop you being shot or blown up … in the hotel. If that happens in the city, it is not my concern.'

Ah, good point!

'What a lovely view! Do you mind if I enjoy it from here for a while?'

The guard was happy to let me sit on the kerb and admire the vista. Way below, the lights of thirty or more tankers twinkled in the bay. Floodlights blinked off in a stadium near the harbour and the streets were quiet, the police having pocketed their whistles for the night.

I took out the bottle and looked to the guard, who didn't seem to mind, though the picture on the label had caught his eye.

'Did Obelix make your wine?' he said, referring to another of Gérard's film roles.

'No,' I said, 'he didn't.'

I thought of elaborating, but felt I should put my feelings behind me. After all, he had helped bring this wine into being, and, as it was one that could alter the world's perception of a wine country severely misjudged, that was a good thing. I'd let things lie, leave the man in peace, and end my quest here.

Besides, I thought, I'd heard a rumour that Clint Eastwood had been seen in a vineyard in Lebanon ...

The Fact File

The following section has been included in the spirit of giving a little more to the knowledge thirsty. Should the details not slake your thirst, I will be delighted to answer any questions that you may have by e-mail:

francis@thewineadventurer.com

Similarly, should you be interested in: a current list of distributors, footage from the trip or The Wine Adventurer free online wine course, please visit the website:

www.thewineadventurer.com

Morocco – Algeria – Tunisia

To say these three countries have similarities is less accurate than to say that there are few things they do not share. The element that most binds them is the Atlas Mountains, and these, almost exclusively, give rise to what separates Morocco, Algeria and Tunisia from the rest of Africa. The countries' shared histories and cultures are veils stretched across the range, the barrier between the Mediterranean and the Sahara, which rises east of Casablanca in Morocco and falls at Tunis, having spanned the entire north of Algeria. Had the countries not the elevation permitted by these often snow-capped peaks, they would largely consist of sand, save for the cooler coastal strips. (Whilst Algeria is predominantly desert, the vast majority of its population is to be found along the coast or in the mountains.)

The Phoenicians, Romans, Vandals, Byzantines, Arabs, Spanish, Ottomans and the French were drawn by the agricultural bounty permitted by cooler elevations in a sunny climate; and whilst the wine history of the Maghreb (the Arabic collective for the three countries) is not as old as the hills, it is as old as the first of these civilisations. It is a history which has seen fortunes wax and wane in a way shared by few other vinegrowing areas. Wine, having been a feature of life from around 1000 BC, fell out of favour with the introduction of Islam in the seventh century, only to be re-introduced by the French in an unprecedented way that rendered the three countries responsible for over 60 per cent of internationally traded wine in the early 1900s.

With the countries' independence in the 1950s and 1960s came a reversal of fortune, leaving the Maghreb again a vinous backwater. The newly installed Islamic powers did not wish to see it promoted internally, and France chose to switch allegiance to her own produce. However, oddly, because of the rise of Islamic fundamentalism, wine is now experiencing a revival. The Muslim governments within each nation have faced (and still do, particularly in Algeria) hard-line opposition from those for whom wine, or rather abstinence, is at the heart of their cause. It seems that governmental defiance, and a drive for overseas revenue, has led to an improvement in the wines, albeit mostly on an export basis to date. However, with 25 to 40 per cent of the Muslim public in the Maghreb consuming alcohol (official figures are sketchy, some implausibly stating zero per cent), there are also substantial home markets to help support a push for development.

The makeup of the vineyards across the three countries is still a hangover from colonial times. They largely contain low-yielding bush vines of the varieties planted by the French (Carignan, Cincault, Grenache and Alicante Bouchet, with a smattering of others), though more recent plantings have been of international varieties (Cabernet Sauvignon, Syrah, Merlot, Mourvèdre, Chardonnay, etc.). These now account for around 20 per cent of the vineyard area. New plantings are largely in Guyot style (trellised) for ease of picking and the increased volumes this method yields, and not for reasons of mechanised harvesting, as almost all grapes are still hand-picked due to the plentiful availability of cheap labour.

There are designated areas across the Maghreb that are considered of higher quality (AOG: Appellation d'Origine Garantie and AOC: Appellation d'Origine Contrôlée), but these delineations are broad and the producer is the more reliable barometer of quality in all cases. When, and if, the industry matures and individual superior plots are singled out, then appellation classifications may become more significant.

Wineries and winemaking practices, of course, differ from producer to producer, though much of the wine is still made in 'caves' (two-storey colonial buildings with banks of cement fermentors above similar cement storage vessels). Whilst some continue to use these out of convenience, others consider them viable because they are seen as no worse than new buildings with stainless steel tanks. (If sanitary conditions are good and temperature control is employed, then this can indeed be the case.) Oak ageing is on the rise, though the expense means that barrels are generally only to be found within higher quality cellars aimed at export markets.

Though the better sites are at cooler altitudes or on the coast, heat in the vineyard and winery is still a hazard for those wishing to produce good wine. However, such obstacles can be overcome by employing hot-climate practices in the vineyards (such as shading the developing grapes with leaf canopy) and diligent temperature control throughout the winemaking process. Whilst there are already good wines emerging, one or two producers are beginning to make great wines. These are coming from the people who have appreciated the conditions and realise that wine should not be made in the same way as in France, but are looking further afield to Australia, Chile and Argentina for inspiration – all warmer countries which, when they first aped the winemaking practices of France, restricted themselves to being considered no more than modest backwaters. Only time will tell whether Algeria, Morocco and Tunisia can follow in such footsteps and reach their true potential, as the political conditions are still, to put it mildly, unfavourable.

Although the three share similar potential, there are some significant differences, such as stage of development, political climate and, importantly, size.

Algeria

Algeria is the country to begin with when considering size. It is impossible to avoid superlatives in a country that could fit most of Western Europe within its borders, and its wine history is one peppered with large numbers too, though these have diminished in 2009 from their peak in the early 1900s: 500 million down to 15 million gallons produced; 400,000 down to 32,000 hectares under vine; 3,000 down to just 70 wineries left. It was once the world's fifth largest wine producer and the biggest exporter, and wine vied with oil for the top spot in export revenue. Most spectators may not mourn the loss of what was mostly bulk wine that poured into France to beef up the lower end of the market, but few stop to consider that this was because the Maghreb 's wines were more palatable than some of the basic French fare at the time. If similar developments that have since taken place in France to improve its own everyday wines were to be applied in Algeria, non-partisan drinkers worldwide could well generate overseas demand again, conditions permitting.

Caught in the eye of the storm during the civil war (1994 – 2002), Algeria's production dwindled to a trickle. It was at the heart of the argument that Islamic militants had with the government. In the early stages of the conflict all of the country's growers were issued with death threats that stated that if they harvested their grapes then they, and their families, would be killed. This led to the closure of 300 wineries and the virtual collapse of the industry. A handful of growers did dare to pick, but the threat wasn't carried out. However there were certainly those killed during the conflict because of their connection with grape growing and winemaking. The government stepped in, further nationalising the vineyards, but also assisting the private growers from whom it still buys (the majority in the country) with loans and grants, as well as providing training to improve vineyard health and grape quality. In addition, the ONCV (Office National de Commercialisation des Produits Viti-vinicoles – the state-owned wine producer) has itself planted over 5,000 hectares of new vineyards with international varieties such as Cabernet Sauvignon, Syrah, Sangiovese and Merlot amongst others, in a bid for exports. The investment has continued into the wineries with a modernisation programme that began in the early 2000s with the installation of chilling equipment and modern presses and pumps. As of 2009 the programme has yet to introduce significant changes to methods of wine storage and transferral (within the wineries and beyond to the new bottling halls) which, if carried out, would undoubtedly further improve quality.

Although the ONCV is thought of as a state monopoly, others have begun to produce and bottle wine, but to date with limited success. That is except for a venture involving a partnership involving Gérard Depardieu, Bernard Magrez and the ONCV. This unfortunately only lasted for one vintage with the release of the 2002 Domaine Saint-Augustin 'Cuvée Monica'. The partnership was dissolved for reasons undisclosed, even though the wine was considered a success (notably by the critic Robert Parker, who awarded it 91-94 points). Its release gave a brief glimpse of what was possible, and there are now plans afoot within the ONCV to emulate its success.

Tunisia

Until the early 2000s, the state of Tunisia's wine industry was broadly similar to that of Algeria, with a virtual state monopoly dominating exports and home markets. Since then an aggressive drive for exports has led to a number of very promising privately-owned partnerships between locals and foreign companies, employing modern methods of vine growing and winemaking. The turnaround owes much to a more enlightened approach by the state owned UCCV (Union Central des Coopératives Viticoles), which began to demonstrate what could be achieved in the late 1990s with a significant modernisation programme.

This move to encourage private producers somewhat mirrors a change in the Moroccan market, where a similar number of partnerships have emerged. However, unlike in Morocco, imports of foreign wines are not allowed, giving home producers access to an internal market without competition. A change of law permitting imports in 2009 may see the advances of these producers a little curtailed, if the not insubstantial home market expresses its curiosity.

The mix of grapes is similar to those of the other two countries, with Carignan, Cincault, Grenache and other traditional varieties making up the bulk planted, largely for gris, rosé and red, though partnerships are also concentrating on international varieties such as Cabernet Sauvignon, Merlot and Syrah, the last of these showing particularly impressive results.

The better vineyards are located within the Cap Bon area, the peninsula to the east of Tunis. Here, some elevation is assisted by a maritime climate, allowing a longer growing season and cooler nights. Mornag is an appellation to look out for, although, as with all three countries, appellation matters less than the name of the producer.

Morocco

Morocco, in terms of volume of quality wine, now leads the Maghreb. The number of overseas partnerships is similar to that in Tunisia, though most are longer established and larger. More significantly, one of the country's best producers is its largest. This is a reversal of the position in the 1990s, where the state accounted for 80 per cent of production. Les Celliers de Meknes, a family-owned concern, has taken the top spot by applying modern methods in the vineyards and wineries, and by treating the home market as being just as important as its exports.

The majority of the best vineyards are situated on a plateau between the low Atlas Mountains and the Zerhoun range, at elevations of 600m to 1,000m, around Meknes and Fes. Also, there are other producers (notably Thalvin) using the cooler coastal climate to their advantage.

The Producers

The following companies are those making the best wines within their respective countries at the time of writing. The order of listing corresponds to the order in which they were visited.

Wines are scored out of a possible 20 points.

Because many of the wines were bottled without vintage indication for the North African market, these have been omitted from the tasting notes. Should you wish more information please visit:

www.thewineadventurer.com

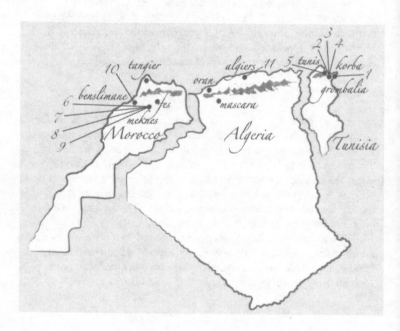

Tunisia

Kurubis

Kurubis is a joint venture between Rhône winemaker Didier Cornillon and a local agribusiness. The enterprise began in 2000 with the planting of vines and building of a modern winery on the outskirts of the coastal town of Korba in Cap Bon. The first wines were made in 2005 and are only for export, with most of the production destined for the French market. Kurubis is modern in its thinking, has a well-equipped winery, and uses organic practices wherever possible in the vineyards. The estate is unusual in making one of Tunisia's two Méthode Traditionnelle sparkling wines.

Map location: 1
Location: Korba, Cap Bon.
Estate size: 21 hectares.

Vineyard
Climate: Maritime. Mediterranean influence.
Soils: Alluvial.
Elevation: 35m.
Varieties: White – Sauvignon, Chardonnay. Red – Syrah, Carignan and Mourvèdre.
Planting: Guyot.

Winery
Fermentation: Stainless steel.
Maturation: Stainless steel.
(225 litre barriques for Kurubis Red and Chardonnay.)
Bottling: Estate bottled.

Tasting Notes
K de Kurubis
100% Chardonnay.
Méthode Traditionnelle.
Nicely balanced wine with clear Chardonnay characters: baked apple,

quince and dried pear. Pleasant wine.
Score: 15.8

Kurubis Chardonnay
10 months in barrique.
Peachy nose, with plenty of creamy oak and tropical aromatics. A little too oaky on the palate but with fruit to support. Medium intensity. Natural style and not confected. Good potential as is from young vines.
Score: 15.3

Kurubis Red
66% Syrah, 34% Mourvèdre.
10 months in French oak.
Purple. Warm plum on the nose with some herbaceous elements and fresh earth backing. Tannic and undeveloped palate, though a little too extracted and a touch thin on fruit. Green elements on the finish. Are they trying to get too much from young vines? Has potential.
Score: 14.8

Domaine Neferis

Nestled in a mountainous amphitheatre in Cap Bon, Domaine Neferis is well sited for the production of quality wine. The slopes channel sea breezes and the elevation gives an extended growing season. Domaine Neferis is the Tunisian land-owning partner. Calatresi, a high quality Sicilian venture, makes the wines. However, the thinking here is Tunisian, with added influence from Australian winemakers helping to gain the best expression from the wines. The estate is progressive in other areas too: the wines are made by Tunisia's only female winemaker, and the winery is experimenting with solar power for its needs.

Map location: 2
Location: Grombalia.
Estate size: 222 hectares.
Production: 400,000 bottles.
Regional classification: AOC Sidi Salem.

Vineyard
Climate: Mediterranean. Hot summers and cool winters.
Soils: Red clay and limestone.
Elevation: 300m to 400m.
Varieties: White – Chardonnay, Pedro Ximenes. Red – Carignan, Grenache, Syrah.
Planting: Old vines – bush; new – Guyot.

Winery
Fermentation: Stainless steel.
Maturation: Stainless steel. Some barrique maturation for upper ranges.
Bottling: Estate bottled.

Tasting Notes
Château Defleur range
Entry-level range made at the winery. AOC Tunisia.

Château Defleur White
50% Pedro Ximenes, 50% Chardonnay.
Pale green in colour. Fresh limey nose with hints of peach and savoury nut. Nicely balanced palate. Limey flavours and savoury cheese rind. Pleasant.
Score: 15.8

Château Defleur Rosé
Grenache.
Lively deep pink. Fresh, simple berry nose, clean and generous. Balanced. Pleasant but simple berry fruit on the palate.
Score: 14.6

Château Defleur Red
50% Carignan, 50% Syrah.
Deep ruby in colour. The nose is a little muted, though showing some cool red fruits and gamey notes. More giving on the palate. Soft tannins supporting ripe plum fruit, and light coffee and chocolate characters from oak.
Score: 15.6

Selian White
70% Chardonnay, 30% Pedro Ximenes.
50% aged in oak.
Medium gold. Quite an intense nose with honeyed characters, pear, acacia and a little oak. Elegant on the palate, though quite powerful, giving and aromatic. Again, honeyed characters over green stone fruit and floral aromatics, rose petal particularly. Fresh, fine and savoury.
Score: 16.8

Selian Rosé
100% Shiraz.
Medicinal style, with bright berry aromatics. Well balanced, fresh and clean, though light on aromatics and not lingering.
Score: 15.0

Selian Red

100% Carignan.

50% oak aged.

Deep, dark and dense. Intense plum, chocolate and damson on the nose. Soft and supple palate with plenty of fine tannins supporting coffee aromas and meaty qualities (fresh not game). Perhaps a little hollow mid-palate. Good persistent length.

Needs time.

Score: 16.0

Selian Reserve

100% old vine Carignan.

100% new oak.

1.5 tonnes per hectare.

Deep, opaque purple. Very intense fruit pastille nose and hints of dark chocolate, though a little dumb otherwise at present. Intense palate. Very plentiful fine tannins. Lots of plummy ripe fruits, chocolate, cinnamon and coffee. Oak nuances are pronounced though the fruit bears it. Again, maybe a touch hollow mid-palate, though that's being picky.

Score: 17.3

Cuvée Magnifique
D'istinto range.

100% Shiraz.

Dark purple. Deep plummy nose. Wild damson, black pepper and macadamia nut. Big palate. Lots of fine tannins, glycerol and acidity supporting. Rich plum jam, chocolate, coffee and spice characters. Tight and yet to fully open, though good potential.

Score: 17.5

Ceptunes

A Tunisian-Swiss enterprise that began in 2002 with the building of a large gravity-fed and highly automated winery in the hills north of Grombalia in Cap Bon. Grapes are sourced from a variety of appellations from contract growers. The winery has unofficial 'Grand Cru' and 'Premier Cru' designations, whereby the title is awarded by an internal tasting panel.

Map location: 3
Location: Grombalia.
Production: 1.2 million bottles.
Regional classification: Largely AOC Sidi Salem, but also AOC Mornag.

Vineyard

Assorted contracts.
Varieties: White – Chardonnay, Sauvignon. Red – Cabernet Sauvignon, Carignan, Grenache, Merlot, Syrah.

Winery

Fermentation: Stainless steel.
Maturation: Stainless steel. Some barrique ageing for the reds.
Bottling: Winery bottled.

Tasting Notes

Jour et Nuit White
80% Chardonnay, 20% Sauvignon.
Clean palate. Fresh and simple, showing some apple fruit and light peach. No oak, little length.
Score: 14.8

2002 Jour et Nuit Red (1st vintage from library stock)
70% Syrah, 20% Merlot, 10% Cabernet Sauvignon.
Ruby red, some orange at the edges. Developed sweet nose with plums, dusty cedar and candied peel. Chunky on the palate with dried red berry characters, cherry and spice. Pleasant and drinkable but now tiring.
Score: 15.6

Didona Chardonnay

Deep straw colour. Clean, fresh nose, though oak dominant over any Chardonnay character. Tropical notes on the palate but two-dimensional overall.
Score: 14.7

Didona Red

80% Syrah, 20% Merlot.
Pale red. High tone plum, some spice, oak smoke and cocoa. Soft palate feel. Medium tannins, fair balance and reasonable length.
Score: 16.0

Didona Reserve Red

90% Syrah, 10% Cabernet Sauvignon.
10 months in oak.
Muted on the nose. Soft palate, some herb, ripe plum and spice. Still closed, but hinting at more depth.
Score: 15.4

Domaine Atlas

This domaine is another recently formed partnership, this time between locals and an Austrian company, though using vineyards from an old estate. Many new varieties were introduced in 2001when the enterprise began, though grapes from old vine Carignan and Syrah provide the juice for the better of the estate's reds.

Map location: 4
Location: Bou Argoub, between Grombalia and Hammamet.
Estate size: 100 hectares.
Regional classification: AOC Mornag.

Vineyard
Climate: Mediterranean. Hot summers and cool winters.
Soils: Clay over limestone.
Elevation: 96m.
Varieties: Whites – Chardonnay, Ugni Blanc, Muscat, Vermentino.
Reds – Cabernet Sauvignon, Carignan (40 years), Mourvèdre, Syrah and Merlot.
Planting: Old vines – bush; new – Guyot.

Winery
Fermentation: Stainless steel.
Maturation: Stainless steel. Barrique for the better wines.
Bottling: Estate bottled.

Tasting Notes
Conducted a tasting from barrique and tank of wines yet to be blended or bottled. Fair potential.

UCCV – Union Central des Coopératives Viticoles 'Les Vignerons de Carthage'

Established in 1948 pre-Independence, UCCV is Tunisia's largest and most important wine producer. Some might choose to overlook the output of anything calling itself a cooperative, though to do so would be to overlook some of Tunisia's best wines. The company is a complex arrangement of state-owned estates and local and international partnerships, which together account for the majority of Tunisia's output. The company is worthy of note for more than statistics alone, as since the early nineties UCCV has invested considerable amounts in modernising everything from the vineyards to the labels, giving the wines a more international style both in taste and presentation. This renaissance is largely the result of efforts by Belgacem D'Khili, the company's Directeur Général. A doctor in viticulture, he began by planting international varieties and changing vineyard practices away from those concerned purely with creating bulk wine.

Map location: 5
Location: Central facility and storage in Tunis, but estates throughout the country.
Estate size: Controls 10,000 hectares (of 17,000 in Tunisia).
Production: 20 million bottles.
Regional classification: Predominantly: AOC 1er Cru Coteaux de Tebourba, AOC Coteaux de Tebourba, AOC Mornag, AOC Grand Cru Mornag, AOC Muscat de Kelibia 1er Cru.

Vineyard

Modern techniques are employed throughout its vineyards and those of contract growers.

Winery

Wineries are large scale and modern (stainless steel), though some have the capacity to produce small batch wines.

Range

A range of wines from entry level to high quality labels for cellaring. 70 per cent of the company's production is rosé and gris, largely for the home market. Only 32 per cent of output is destined for export.

Tasting Notes

2001 Vieux Magon AOC Mornag

60% Carignan (50 years), 40% Syrah.

Deep red to purple. Warm brooding nose with good depth of fruit. Supple plummy notes, oak and figs, and secondary aromatics: dusty spices and dry earth. Voluptuous palate. Plenty of fine tannins. Rich, viscous and balanced. Not too alcoholic. Fine and persistent with dried berries and cherry on length. Still lively.

Score: 17.3

2002 Vieux Magon AOC Mornag

60% Carignan (50 years), 40% Syrah.

Deeply coloured and more purple than 2001. Fresher nose than 2001 too. Again plummy in style. Syrah influence showing with medicine, spices and pepper over berry fruit. Big on the palate. Plentiful tannins, though not as developed in flavour. A hint of green overlaying, but still very good. Fresher and more primary flavour. Needs time. I prefer it, but he says the 2001was considered the classic.

Score: 17.6 plus one smiley face.

1976 and **1986** Vieux Magon are both apparently still drinking well.

Domaine Clipea Chardonnay

Gold. Clean, international style. Appealing. Light oak over crisp nectarine on the nose. Fresh, apple fruits on the palate, nicely balanced and not overly rich. Pleasant and quite elegant. Light peachy finish.

Score: 15.6

Magon Rosé

Cincault, Grenache.

Fresh pink colour. Savoury nose. Simple berry aromas. Pleasant, crisp and cleansing.

Score: 15.0

Muscat de Kelibia

AOC 1er Cru Kelibia.

Light straw colour. Lively Muscat nose with mouth-watering grapey aromatics and tropical fruits hinting at sweetness. Clean and pleasing. Perfectly dry palate. A little musk and earthy notes over fruit. Clean acidic style, though losing character mid-palate. Short length.
Score: 14.5

Sidi Saad

Grand Cru Mornag.

Carignan, Syrah, Mourvèdre.

Ruby red. Gently aged nose. Light pleasant berry characters and secondary aromatics. Pleasant palate feel. Clean acidity. Simple and flavoursome, but losing a little fruit mid-palate and a touch dry on the finish. Losing flesh but still enjoyable.
Score: 15.2

Les Domaines de Carthage Syrah

Medium red. Farmyard nose. A little funky but not unpleasant. Some light spice. Medium rich palate, chunky red fruit, a hint of volatile acidity and CO_2.
Score: 13.4

Les Domaines de Carthage Merlot

Medium red, purple hint. Muted nose. A little stemmy. Palate better with a pleasing balance. Quite chunky to voluptuous feel. Cherry, plum, black fruits and hints of earth.
Score: 14.6

Les Domaines de Carthage Pinot Noir

Pale red. Light, warm nose. A little sweet. Cherry. Soft light palate. Strawberry jam, light herb, raisin notes.
Score: 14.3

Morocco

Castel

The Castel property is centred on an old colonial stud farm built outside Meknes in the 1920s. The French-Moroccan partnership, started in the early nineties, hasn't changed the nature of the original setting except by adding a few functional buildings to the rear, and a relaxed atmosphere belies a highly organised and professional enterprise within. The operation comprises five estates, covering the AOC Guerrouane and Beni M'Tir appellations, most of which are at an altitude of over 600 metres, giving a prolonged growing season. Methods here are distinctly French and the emphasis is on producing clean modern wines for export markets.

Map location: 6
Location: Meknes.
Estate size: 1,200 hectares.
Regional classification: AOG Guerrouane, AOG Beni M'Tir.

Vineyard
Climate: Hot summers and cold winters.
Soils: Reds – red clay and limestone. Whites and gris – sandy.
Elevation: 650m.
Varieties: Reds (85% of production) – Cabernet Sauvignon, Grenache, Merlot, Syrah. Gris – Cincault. Whites – Grenache Blanc, Semillon and Vermentino.
Planting: Guyot.

Winery
Fermentation: Stainless steel.
Maturation: Stainless steel.
Bottling: Modern bottling facility on site.

Tasting Notes

Castel Domaine de Sahari Gris

Cincault, Grenache Blanc.

Pale onion skin. Light intensity on the nose. Sweet apple, candied fruits, strawberry. Medium depth palate but a little light on flavour. Spritzy acidity. Fair wine, but not very interesting.

Score: 14.6

Castel Domaine de Sahari Réserve White

100% Grenache Blanc.

Pale straw. Fresh, medium intensity nose. Cox apple, white plum and citrus. Rich palate, savoury nut characters, baked apple. Medium acidity. Not bad, but lacking freshness and a little oily on the finish.

Score: 14.9

Castel Domaine de Sahari Cabernet Merlot

Cabernet Sauvignon, Merlot.

Clear medium red. Pronounced nose. Simple warm red fruits, cinnamon and green pepper. Medium bodied palate, but tannins a bit too grippy now, though they should mellow. Green pepper characters over simple blueberry fruit. Short finish.

Score: 15.0

Castel Domaine Larroque Gris

Very pale salmon pink. Muted nose. Simple blossom and light herb over berries. Chunky palate, though has acidity to cope. Simple strawberry fruit style. Fair quaffing wine.

Score: 14.8

Castel Domaine Larroque White

Medium yellow, gold tints. Fresh nose. Nectarine & lemon. Savoury nut hints beneath white stone fruits and baked apple on the palate. Reasonable length, but quite an oily finish. A little too warm.

Score: 14.5

Castel Domaine Mayole Cabernet Sauvignon Syrah
Deep red, purple hue. Restrained nose, hinting at depth. Black cherry, blackcurrant and spice on the nose. Chunky, pleasing palate. Blackcurrant, red pepper and roasted nut. Grippy tannins with viscosity to match. Interesting wine.
Score: 16.3

Castel l'Excellence de Bonnassia Cabernet Sauvignon Merlot
Deep red to purple. Generous nose. Raspberry and plums over red meat. Fleshy palate, fresh plum jam, currant and green pepper. Cool, viscous and grippy, but tannins yet to soften. A well made, interesting wine.
Score: 16.5

Castel Halana Merlot
Pale cherry red. Medium intensity nose. Raspberry jam and tar. Hot, medium bodied, palate. Light overboiled strawberry jam. Tannins a little bitter. Sugary length. A little clumsy.
Score: 13.8

Castel Halana Syrah
Deep red. Medium intensity nose. Simple plum jam style. Hot palate. Sweetish body. Medium tannins. Low acidity. Boiled cherry, some spice. Simple.
Score: 14.2

Volubilia – Domaine de la Zouina

The company's literature states that the two French partners, Gérard Gribelin (ex Ch Fieuzal) and Philippe Gervoson (Larrivet Haut-Brion) fell in love with the soils of the area on a golf trip in 2001. They must have thrown their clubs away and begun work immediately, as by 2002 they had formed a partnership (Volubilia) with Domaine de la Zouina and planted 63 hectares of vines. The seriousness with which they are approaching the venture indicates a level of understanding of the potential of the region that many are unaware of. Great care is being taken in the vineyards; indeed, as much as at their properties in Bordeaux (although the methods are in tune with local conditions) and much effort is dedicated to extracting maximum potential from the estate. Domaine de la Zouina is currently managed by Gérard Gribelin's son, Christophe, and the vineyard management and winemaking is in the hands of Philippe Lespy, formerly of Domaines Barons de Rothschild. The first vintage was in 2005 and since then the wines have won a number of accolades and are set to improve year on year.

Map location: 7
Location: El Hajeb, Meknes.
Estate size: 63 hectares of vines increasing to 115 hectares with new plantings.
Production: 350,000 bottles.
Regional classification: AOG Guerrouane.

Vineyard

Climate: Hot summers and cool winters.
Soils: Clay and limestone. Gravel in parts.
Elevation: 800m.
Varieties: Whites – Chardonnay. Rosé – Caladoc, Marselan. Gris – Mourvèdre, Tempranillo. Red – Cabernet Sauvignon, Syrah, Tempranillo.
Planting: Guyot. No herbicides or pesticides used, though not fully organic yet.

Winery

Gravity-fed winery.

Fermentation: Epoxy resin lined cement tanks.

Maturation: Period in barrique for premium labels and gris and rosé.

Bottling: Estate bottled.

Tasting Notes

Volubilia Gris

Mourvèdre, Tempranillo.

Pale onion skin. Fresh, aromatic nose. Delicate, ripe peach and floral notes. Elegant and serious. Crisp palate. Crunchy acidity. Mineral notes. Mouth-watering white stone fruits and blossom. Very good indeed.

Score: 16.9

Volubilia Rosé

Caladoc, Marselan, Syrah.

Vibrant rose-pink. Savoury on the nose, a serious style. Redcurrant and whiffs of jam over dried herb. More weighty than the gris, though lively acidity through it all. Mineral elements. Plenty of length. Very well made.

Score: 16.7

Volubilia Red

45% Cabernet Sauvignon, 20% Syrah, 25% Tempranillo, 10% Mourvèdre. Dark cherry colour. Intense nose of blackcurrant and cherry, with hints of smoke and meat. Big supple palate. Fine tannins. Soft but not too sweet. Ripe red fruits, hints of herb, musk and spice. Very good.

Score: 17.0

Epicuria Chardonnay

Deep yellow to gold. Warm tropical nose. Enticing and complex (best of what the US used to do). Custard and dessert apple. Crisp palate. Big and attention-grabbing but complex nonetheless. Sweet apple, quince and green almonds with a meaty musk. Viscous and cool through the palate.

Score: 17.3

Epicuria Syrah – Tank sample

Purple. Big organic nose. Wild meat, truffle, smoke and plum jam. Very sweet fruits on palate, plum jam, boiled strawberry and roasted red pepper. Fine, plentiful tannins. Berry fruits, hints of angelica, ginger. Medium weight on finish. Very good.
Score: 17.1

Epicuria Cabernet Sauvignon – Tank sample

Deep red. Sweet blueberry nose. Chocolate hints. Ripe. Warm palate, a little too much so, though some grip. Super ripe berry. Overcooked.
Score: 14.5

Tempranillo – Tank sample

Pale cherry red. Deep smoky nose. Stone fruits. Soft palate. Again quite hot, sweet red berries, Syrah-like, plus a little oak spice. No great length at moment. Closed.
Score: 15.5

Château Roslane – Celliers de Meknes

Celliers de Meknes is the country's largest producer creating wines at all price points from five estates. With over 50 years of vinegrowing and winemaking experience, Rene Zniber, the owner, is largely regarded as the founder of the renaissance of Moroccan wine. His passion and drive for quality is nowhere more apparent than at Château Roslane, the company's flagship estate situated in Morocco's only Appellation d'Origine *Contrôlée* region, AOC Coteaux d'Atlas. Château Roslane is immaculate throughout, from the neatly manicured gardens, fountains and riad, to the technologically advanced winery including an underground barrel cellar with a capacity for 3,000 barriques. A range of premium brands is also made at Château Roslane alongside the Château Roslane 1er Cru White and Red.

Map location: 8
Location: Meknes.
Estate size: Château Roslane – 700 hectares.
(Celliers de Meknes – 2100 hectares over five estates in total.)
Production: Château Roslane – 9 million bottles.
(Celliers de Meknes – 27 million bottles.)
Regional classification: Château Roslane – AOC Coteaux d'Atlas 1er Cru.

Vineyard

Climate: Mainly continental with hot summers and cool winters. Cool nights.
Soils: Château Roslane – clay over limestone.
Elevation: All estates are between 580 and 700 metres.
Varieties: Château Roslane 1er Cru: White – Chardonnay. Red – Cabernet Sauvignon, Merlot and Syrah. Many other varieties are grown for the other brands.
Planting: Château Roslane – Guyot. Others – bush and Guyot.

Winery

Château Roslane: state-of-the-art gravity-fed winery.
Fermentation: Château Roslane 1er Cru White – barrique. Château Roslane 1er Cru Red – stainless steel.
Maturation: Barrique for both red and white.
Bottling: Estate bottled.

Tasting Notes

Trois Domaines White

AOG Gerrouane.

Ugni Blanc, Clairette, Sauvignon.

Pale green. Fresh apple and pear nose with light floral notes. Crisp palate. Pleasing primary aromas. A well-made, simple wine.

Score: 15.4

Trois Domaines Rosé

AOG Gerrouane.

50% Cincault, 50% Grenache.

Medium red. Light nose. Gentle fresh berry style. Crisp palate. Correct. Generally berry-like but short and simple.

Score: 14.2

Trois Domaines Red

Cincault, Grenache, Carignan, Alicante Bouchet.

Medium red. Warmed leather and plum sweets on the nose. Simple but pleasant. Good weight on palate, not too reliant on sugar. Berry jam.

Score: 14.9

Riad Jamil White

100% Chardonnay.

Light yellow. A little spritz. High acidity. Green peach characters. OK but lacking much of interest.

Score: 14.5

Riad Jamil Rosé

100% Syrah.

Pale purple. Serious on the nose, savoury aromas over berry. Chunky red-black fruits and meaty notes. Dry and fine. Good extract.

Score: 16.0

Riad Jamil Red

100% Carignan. (40-year-old vines.)

Medium red. Sweet fruit pastille nose, tobacco, tar and black cherry. Supple palate, balanced and surprisingly grippy. Not over hot. Still needs time, but already complex and interesting aromatically.

Score: 16.9

Ksar Rosé

100% Cabernet Sauvignon.

Light reddish hue. Pronounced, sweet currant fruit. Pleasant. Some bubble gummy notes, cherry sweets. Fun and quaffable.

Score: 15.5

Ksar Red

70% Cabernet Sauvignon, 30% Syrah.

Red purple hints. Berry fruits and sweet plum on the nose. Soft, quite fine on palate. Small-grain tannins. Plenty of character: plum, tobacco, sweet cherry and prune.

Score: 16.3

Château Roslane Premier Cru White

100% Chardonnay.

Deep yellow to gold. Ripe vanilla nose over sweet peach and nectarine. Gentle musk. Soft buttery palate. Oak a little pronounced now. Mineral and greener fruit qualities. Should soften. Good.

Score: 16.5

Château Roslane Premier Cru Red

Cabernet Sauvignon, Merlot, Syrah.

Intense nose: boiled plums, cassis and hints of oak smoke, chocolate and roast pepper. We got into a protracted conversation regarding wine and religion when I was about to make notes on the palate, and I forgot to put my thoughts down, or the glass for that matter. I remember it as being good though, probably around 17ish.

Les Deux Domaines

This is the name by which the Franco-Moroccan partnership involving Gérard Depardieu is titled in Morocco. As well as the Moroccan landowners (who are renting the land from the King on a 60-year lease) and Gérard Depardieu, the partnership includes another French element and a highly influential one, that of the Bordeaux kingpin Bernard Magrez. It is in no small part his experience and the resources of a wine empire numbering over 26 highly reputed properties worldwide that have allowed the estate to produce such a world-class wine in a short space of time. The estate has been lavished with all it needs, but above all it has a simplicity allowed by those who understand the environment and how to obtain the best from it: through non-intervention, allowing the wine its own expression. The estate in effect only creates one wine, a blend of Syrah with the addition of Grenache, all planted in the early nineties with the intention of releasing a wine in the mid 2000s once the vines reached adequate maturity. Bernard Magrez bottles the wine under Gérard Depardieu's 'Lumière' label, as well as 'Kahina'. There are new plantings for a white and gris, which have yet to reach maturity.

Map location: 9
Location: Meknes.
Estate size: 64 hectares.
Regional classification: AOG Guerrouane.

Vineyard
Climate: Hot summers and cold winters. Frost sometimes a problem.
Soils: Sandy.
Elevation: 700m.
Varieties: 25 hectares Syrah and 10 hectares Grenache.
29 hectares newly planted Chardonnay, Vermentino and Alicante Bouchet for white and gris.
Planting: Guyot.

Winery
Fermentation: Wooden cuvées (Lumière) and stainless steel.
Maturation: 100% new barrique for Syrah. 100% new oak hogsheads for Grenache.
Bottling: Estate bottled.

Range

Kahina – Bernard Magrez label.
Lumière – Gérard Depardieu label.

Tasting Notes: Barrel Samples

Syrah

The following lots represent the entire production of 2007 Syrah and are from the same vineyard, but different fermentation batches. All had spent ten months in new French oak at the time of tasting.

2007 Syrah (Lot 3) – from barrel

Dark purple. Jammy nose. Intense black cherry, then plenty of spicy vanilla and roasted coffee from the oak. Big and brooding. Pleasing too. Powerful palate. Huge amounts of tannin – both oak and grape, yet very supple. Plenty of primary fruits underlying the oak influence: damson jelly, red plum, black cherry, hints of almond, then spices and a gunflint minerality. Excellent.
Score: 17.5

2007 Syrah (Lot 1) – from barrel

Dark purple. A little dumber on the nose, hints of medicine through the cherry. Palate softer and fruitier. Sweeter. Fine tannins – lighter than Lot 3. Lighter spices, coriander over plummy fruits. Elegant. Very good.
Score: 17.0

2007 Syrah (Lot 2) – from barrel

Dark purple. Dumb on the nose, brooding. Bigger palate than Lot 1. More viscous with large globs of tannins and glycerol. Aromatic characters similar to 3, though a little more muted. Very good.
Score: 17.3

2007 Grenache – from barrel

Rich cherry red. Raisin cake, dried fruit, candied peel and caramel and toffee. Lovely! Big chunky palate, spirity prune liqueur. Roship. Soft, fleshy and decadent.
Score: 16.9

Fact File - The Producers

The first blend – the three Syrah wines
The three lots of Syrah blended together in equal parts.
Soft, balanced and warm. Predictably somewhere between the three in character.

The final blend – the three Syrah wines, plus Grenache
66% Syrah (the first blend), 33% Grenache.
Deep red to purple. Soft, ripe and rich with plentiful aromatics. The best of all these wines. Plenty of varied and changing aromatics: a blend of black fruits, spices and fruit syrup. Rosehip and angelica on the finish. Persistent and powerful.
Score: 17.6

Older Releases - from bottle.

2003 Kahina – Bernard Magrez label
66% Syrah, 33% Grenache.
Dark curranty purple centre, tawny edges. Big chocolaty nose, plenty of new wood mingling with damson jam and cinnamon spice. Chunky palate with bags of fleshy stone fruits and other primary fruit aromatics. Still fresh. Vanilla, violets and spice on the length.
Score: 17.3

2002 Lumière – Gérard Depardieu label
66% Syrah, 33% Grenache.
Deep cherry red, tawny.
Dried, dusty cherry and strawberry on the nose, overlaid by spice and tinderwood. Rich hot palate. Big and grippy mouthfeel with plum jam, tar and spice aromatics. Not as elegant as Kahina. Now a touch too hot and a little past its best. Tasted one year on from the Graham Norton show, after the trip.
Score: 16.6

These older wines were the first releases, made from grapes selected from vineyards other than Les Deux Domaines. The newer wines show a greater potential for ageing due to higher acidities and lower levels of alcohol.

Thalvin / Domaine des Ouled Thaleb

Domaine des Ouled Thaleb, the land-based Moroccan half of this partnership, dates from 1927, when 3,000 hectares of vines were planted at Ben Slimane. The estate is smaller today: only 400 hectares of vines remain at the original site, but the winery can boast that it is the oldest still in use in the country. Thalvin joined them in 1968, making it one of the oldest partnerships too. The estate draws on two other vineyards inland, giving diversity of climates and soils for the wide range of varieties planted. These give an equally varied range of wines from entry level to premium. New 'garage' bottlings using old vine stock are planned. Though original cement tanks are in use this is out of preference (new cement vats are being built) and the thinking here is modern and market-driven.

Map location: 10
Location: Ben Slimane.
Estate size: 1,060 hectares approx. Both coastal and new plantings inland. Plus contracts with growers.
Production: 3.5 million bottles.

Vineyard
Climate: Coast – warm maritime. Inland – warm continental.
Soils: Coast – sandy. Inland – clay and limestone.
Elevation: Coast – 80m. Inland – 600m.
Varieties: Red – Cabernet Sauvignon, Cabernet Franc, Grenache, Marselan, Merlot, Pinot Noir, Syrah, Tempranillo.
White – Chardonnay, Chenin, Clairette, Farranah, Ricot, Sauvignon, Ugni Blanc, Viognier.
Planting: Mostly Guyot. Some old bush vines.

Winery
Fermentation: Cement vats.
Maturation: Cement. Barrique for top labels.
Bottling: Estate bottled.

Range

Cuvée du Président Red, White and Rosé.
Siroua Red, White and Gris.
S de Siroua Red, White and Rosé.
Médaillon Red, White and Rosé.
CB Initiales Red and White.
Tandem.

Tasting Notes

Cuvée du Président White

Clairette, Ugni Blanc, Farranah.
Pale straw. Fresh nose, light blossom. Crisp and balanced. Medium weight. Light and savoury.
Score: 14.3

Première du Président Rosé

Cincault, Grenache, Syrah.
Pale pink. A little muted (recently bottled). Fresh strawberry, rosehip and herb. Some C02. Good structuring acidity. A little closed but some strawberry and savoury notes. Potentially good, but needs a little time.
Score: 16.0

Première du Président Red

Cabernet Sauvignon, Grenache.
Deep red. Green pepper nose, herbaceous Cabernet notes, some mint and parsley. Soft palate. Warm. A little sugar. Tight tannins. A little leafy, some earth and red fruit. OK.
Score: 15.5

Siroua Gris

100% Cincault.
Pale pinky orange. Sweet bubble gum on the nose. Fresh jammy fruits beneath. Like entering a sweet shop. Clean acidity, plenty of fleshy fruits. Bonbon Anglais.
Score: 16.0

S de Siroua White
100% Chardonnay.
Medium yellow. A little spritz on the appearance. Lively acidity. Peach and apple flavours, but no further layers of Chardonnay character. Pleasant wine, but there could be more to it.
Score: 15.8

S de Siroua Red
Inky black. Damson and tar on the nose. Soft, silky palate. Plenty of integrated tannin, rounded.
Score: 16.7

Médaillon Sauvignon
Pale straw. Hint of sulphur. Pleasant nose. Hints of grass and greengage. Not a classic Sauvignon. Green plums and crisp apple, but few hints of Sauvignon. Nice enough wine though.
Score: 15.6

Médaillon Rosé
100% Syrah.
Vibrant pink. Fresh nose. Balanced palate. Fresh berries, some cough mixture and strawberry.
Score: 16.2

Médaillon Red
Cabernet, Syrah, Merlot.
Dark red. Warm, plummy nose. Cherry and a little tar. Syrah influence. Soft, sweet palate. Fine tannins. Good balance, but not very complex. Tight finish. The wine is mostly structure at the moment and needs time, but I'm not convinced it has the aromatics to last.
Score: 16.4

CB (Cuvée barrique) White
100% Chardonnay.
Gold colour. Vanilla oak over grape characters. Peach, lemon. Bigger palate, pleasant creamy feel. Enjoyable aromatics from barrique, though too much over the wine's character. Oak dominates after initial sips, its character is too strong.
Score: 15.3

CB (Cuvée barrique) Red
100% Cabernet Sauvignon. (40-year-old vines.)
Medium red. Distinctive Cabernet nose. Currant fruits, some mint leaf. Soft, sweet and quite extracted. Hot on the mid-palate, greenish and nervy on the finish. At present structure wins over aromatics. Doubtful that aromas will last.
Score: 16.5

Old Vine Syrah. (From barrel.)
Dark purple. Deep and smoky: grape dominant above oak, farmyard hints. Fine, powerful tannins, sweet black cherry, ripe plums and prune influence, lovely palate feel and persistent aromatics.
Score: 17.4

Syrah 60-year-old vines. (From barrel.)
Dark purple. Deep nose. Tarry, damson jam, mixed spice, dried fruits. Huge tannins, both wood and wine. Globs of dry extract and plenty of aromatics: cherry, chocolate, spices, tobacco and angelica.
Score: 18.0

Tandem
100% Syrah.
Deep red, purple hints. A real Rhône nose. Remarkably the same cigar smoke as a good Cornas. Restrained, very interesting, subtle and elegant. Medicinal, pepper and bitter damson. Coolish characters. Medium to full weight.
Score: 17.3

Le Val d'Argan

Although not visited as a part of the trip, details of this small estate came to light while travelling and were considered worthy of inclusion after a tasting of the whites. The property is owned and governed by Charles Melia of Château de la Font du Loup in Châteauneuf-du-Pape. He founded the estate in 1994 on the coast near Essaouira, making it the most southerly quality winery in the Maghreb. The latitude is hot but the climate is tempered by Atlantic breezes and the quality of the wine indicates a fair understanding of hot climate winemaking.

Location: Essaouira.
Estate size: 30 hectares.
Production: 120,000 bottles.

Vineyard

Climate: Hot maritime.
Soils: Clay and limestone.
Varieties: Exclusively Rhône varieties.
Red – Grenache, Mourvèdre, Syrah.
White – Bourboulenc, Clairette, Muscat, Roussanne, Ugni Blanc.
Planting: Guyot. Organic status.

Winery

Fermentation: Cement vats.
Maturation: Cement. Barrique for top labels.
Bottling: Estate bottled.

Tasting Notes

Le Val d'Argan Mogador White
Blend of the white varieties.
Deep yellow to gold. Savoury nose, nut, cheese rind and quince. Fleshy palate. Nuts, cheddar and dried apple. Warm but not too hot. Fair acidity backing medium alcohol. Honey on the finish. Good wine. Score: 16.5

Le Val d'Argan Grande Réserve White

100% Roussanne.

Gold. High intensity nose. Ripe melon, fig, cheese rind, honey and a hint of vanilla oak. Chunky palate, warm and mouth-coating. Good balance. Dried peach, toffee apple and integrated oak. A big, interesting wine with plenty of character.

Score: 17.0

Le Val d'Argan Mogador Red

Blend of the red varieties.

Dark red. Muted nose. Redcurrant and dusty wood. Astringent palate, tannins aggressive and overpowering. Cool feel. Aromatics a little dumb. Hints of currants, damson and tar, but lost within the structure.

Score: 14.2

Le Val d'Argan Grande Réserve Red

Blend of the red varieties.

Opaque red. Gamey nose, black pepper & kirsch. Palate again dominated by tannin, more balanced but still astringent. Interesting aromatics, damson, cedar and blackcurrant, but they will be gone by the time the tannins soften.

Score: 15.0

Algeria

ONCV

Formed in 1968 after independence from France, the story of the state-owned ONCV (Office National de Commercialisation des Produits Viti-vinicoles) is that of the Algerian wine industry: one of diminishing fortunes now just again on the rise. The company is the only exporter of wine and accounts for over 80 per cent of the country's vineyard area, comprising owned land and contracts with growers (who, in turn, lease from the state). This has enabled the company to play a large part in governing vineyard practices with contractors. The company is also in the unique position worldwide of having access to so many formerly-identified high quality plots (many with old vines) but at present the grapes from these are blended with fruit from lesser sites to form standard labels. This may change in the future however, as the company has adopted a more forward thinking approach since the nineties in order to increase export markets. A far-reaching modernisation programme, including the planting of international varieties and the installation of modern equipment within its wineries, is under way, and organic status has been granted at a number of sites. There is also talk of producing small batch wines, which will only help highlight the vast potential, which is, as yet, barely tapped. This could be the Penfolds of North Africa, when, and if, commercial conditions allow.

Map location: 11
Location: Countrywide.
Estate size: 5,000 hectares owned. 28,000 hectares contracted.
Production: 50 million bottles.

Vineyard

Climate: Maritime to continental.
Soils: Wide ranging.
Elevation: 20m to 900m.
Varieties: Traditional – Carignan, Cincault, Grenache. New – Chardonnay, Cabernet Sauvignon, Merlot, Sangiovese, Syrah.
Planting: Traditional – bush. Modern – Guyot.

Winery

Fermentation: 16 wineries with cement tanks.
Maturation: Cement tanks.
Bottling: Centralised bottling plants.

Range

Cuvée du Président. (No connection to Thalvin's bottling of the same name.)
Coteaux de Tlemcen AOG (4 labels).
Coteaux de Mascara AOG (3 labels).
Dahra AOG (3 labels).
Coteaux du Zaccar AOG.
Media AOG (3 labels).
Varietal range.

Tasting Notes

Syrah

Good cherry colour. Bright. Warm fruits, pleasant berry style. Medium intensity. Medium weight. Good fruit, nice fruity Syrah character. Boiled berries.
Score: 14.7

Media

Carignan, Cincault, Grenache.
Dark red, some purple. Medium nose. Clean fruits, some red berry and black cherry. Medium weight. Fruity and warm palate. Spiced cherry fruits.
Score: 15.2

Media – Château Tellagh

Carignan, Cincault, Grenache.
Good colour, a little developed. Clean berry nose. Warm, a touch mulled. Fine tannins. Meaty qualities over cherry and blackberry fruits. Clean and well made, but a little hot.
Score: 15.8

Sangiovese

Rosy red, orange hints. Light. Cherry nose. Warm palate. Pastille fruits, red berry, hints of sweet spice. Some herb. Jammy style.
Score: 15.8

Dahra

Carignan, Cincault, Grenache.
Medium red. Tight nose. Clean berry, light spice. Rich palate. Good tannins. Nice feel, fresh and warm. Quite perfumed.
Score: 15.6

Coteaux de Mascara – Domaine el Bordj

Good deep colour, some development. Closed nose. Black cherry nuances. Fair tannin integration. Persistent & warm but not too much so.
Score: 16.2

Coteaux de Mascara – Château Feres

Carignan, Cincault, Grenache.
Lighter than the other Mascara. Warm cherry notes. Soft tannins. Herbs and hints of berry. Fair.
Score: 14.8

Cuvée du Président

Dark red to purple. Black fruits, cherry and plum, a hint of herb and a bit of funk. Big and chunky palate but a little too alcoholic. Extracted. Big, but the aromatics don't quite justify the structure. Greenish hints, early sugar harvest. Still, better than the Oran bottle.
Score: 15.2

2002 Domaine de Saint Augustin Cuvée Monica
Gérard Depardieu, Bernard Magrez, ONCV

Orange red, tawny. Warm nose with plenty of interesting aromatics: damson jelly, pastilles and cedar, hints of tar. Showing its age. Palate viscous and jammy, but fruits now receding to expose alcohol and tertiary aromatics of earth and dusty wood. Hinting at former glory.
16.3